Violence

Using discourses from across the conceptual and geographical board, Toby Miller argues for a different way of understanding violence, one that goes beyond supposedly universal human traits to focus instead on the specificities of history, place, and population as explanations for it.

Violence engages these issues in a wide-ranging interdisciplinary form, examining definitions and data, psychology and ideology, gender, nation-states, and the media by covering several foundational questions:

- how has violence been defined, historically and geographically?
- has it decreased or increased over time?
- which regions of the world are the most violent?
- does violence correlate with economies, political systems, and religions?
- what is the relationship of gender and violence?
- what role do the media play?

This book is a powerful introduction to the study of violence, ideal for students and researchers across the human sciences, most notably sociology, American and area studies, history, media and communication studies, politics, literature, and cultural studies.

Toby Miller is Stuart Hall Professor of Cultural Studies, Universidad Autónoma Metropolitana–Cuajimalpa; Research Professor of the Graduate Division, University of California, Riverside; and Sir Walter Murdoch Distinguished Collaborator, Murdoch University. He is the author and editor of 50 books and hundreds of articles and chapters.

'With characteristic geographical breadth and linguistic *élan*, Toby Miller fuses a remarkable range of disciplines and examples to consider the meaning of violence in its many permutations—from rape and domestic violence through to school shootings and the "slow violence" of ecological destruction. Stacked with startling statistics, *Violence* is both a lively generator of debate and a visceral argument against the destructiveness of patriarchy, religion, capitalism and war.'

Jo Littler, *City, University of London, UK*

'Miller's famously capacious mind is working at full throttle in this tour de force book. *Violence* delivers analyses and insights that will unsettle readers, and stick with them for a long time.'

Andrew Ross, *New York University, USA*

'This immensely readable book takes the reader on a trip through some of the many battlegrounds in which various forms of violence are played out: in an array of grisly statistics, in our brains, in deep-rooted misogyny, in nationalist politics, in journalism and in fiction. The journey is often uncomfortable and always thought-provoking: Miller shows how violence can be sporadic but it is also systemic, and Miller weaves storytelling with social science—combining advocacy with analytical dexterity—to ask where it comes from and who benefits from it.'

Justin Lewis, *Cardiff University, UK*

Violence

Toby Miller

Routledge
Taylor & Francis Group
LONDON AND NEW YORK

First published 2021
by Routledge
2 Park Square, Milton Park, Abingdon, Oxon OX14 4RN

and by Routledge
52 Vanderbilt Avenue, New York, NY 10017

Routledge is an imprint of the Taylor & Francis Group, an informa business

British Library Cataloguing-in-Publication Data
A catalogue record for this book is available from the British Library

Library of Congress Cataloging-in-Publication Data
Names: Miller, Toby, 1958– author.
Title: Violence / Toby Miller.
Description: 1 Edition. | New York : Routledge, 2020. | Includes
    bibliographical references and index.
Identifiers: LCCN 2020020048 (print) | LCCN 2020020049 (ebook) |
    ISBN 9780367197605 (hardback) | ISBN 9780429243110 (ebook)
Subjects: LCSH: Violence. | Violence—Psychological aspects. |
    Violence—Social aspects. | Violence—Political aspects.
Classification: LCC HM1116 .M545 2020 (print) | LCC HM1116
    (ebook) | DDC 303.6—dc23
LC record available at https://lccn.loc.gov/2020020048
LC ebook record available at https://lccn.loc.gov/2020020049

ISBN: 978-0-367-19760-5 (hbk)
ISBN: 978-0-429-24311-0 (ebk)

Typeset in Times New Roman
by Apex CoVantage, LLC

Contents

Acknowledgments

I'd like to thank Akuavi Adonon, Pal Ahluwalia, Luis Albornoz, Dave Andrews, Paulina Aroch, Jesús Arroyave, Mike Butterworth, Ben Carrington, André Dorcé, James Faubion, Natalie Foster, Des Freedman, Trinidad García, Faye Ginsburg, Bill Grantham, Maggie Gray, Brían Hanrahan, Gholam Khiabany, Micah Kleit, Geoff Lawrence, Tom Lutz, Rick Maxwell, Vicki Mayer, Ian McDonald, Jim McKay, Marta Milena, Caitlin Miller, Lainey Paloma Miller, Aurélien Mondon, Thomas Oates, Abeyamí Ortega, Rune Ottosen, Mauro Porto, Tom Reese, Adriana Reygadas, Luis Reygadas, Andrew Ross, David Rowe, Horst Ruthrof, Alfredo Sabbagh, Olga Lucía Sorzano, Imre Szeman, Anamaria Tamayo-Duque, Gavan Titley, Graeme Turner, Aimée Vega, Jennifer Vennall, Jaap Verheul, Berit von der Lippe, Emma Waterton, George Yúdice, and all the workers involved in the production of this book.

Introduction

I've been physically attacked by strangers, though not with lasting impact: socked in the mouth and hit by a brick wandering down mid-morning mean streets; threatened with being thrown from a roof (by a mid-level bureaucrat who was angered to learn that I earned a third of her salary while being a mere academic, and sans her job security); slapped at a party ('You look arrogant' was the explanation, from a person I had never met); and told 'Don't move or I'll shoot' by a police officer while walking through a park. When I was a teenager, my mother assaulted me with a knife—something I didn't think about for two decades. A pal of a then girlfriend once threatened to 'cut your throat' if I ever upset her. When I discussed this with my partner, she told me 'Either he didn't say it, it was a joke, or you deserved it.' So I know what it is to be assaulted, intimidated—and ridiculed about it. That is probably true for many readers of this book.

I have never hit, kicked, slapped, stabbed, shot, sexually assaulted, or poisoned anyone; nor have I caused ongoing physical harm. But I have also twice *been* violent. Biting. I think I reached the limits of that violence three decades ago. It was a shock to me then, as it is now. Some very simple counseling techniques, added to pre-existing political awareness, put an end to it. Knowing one is capable of such things can be an ongoing aid to restricting their realization. But I clearly have the potential lurking within.

I remain by turns appalled and attracted by news coverage and dramatizations of violence. I cannot watch screen texts where a stalker's point of view depicts hunting a woman; I abjure the horror genre; and I don't like novels that go into grisly detail about injuries. But by choice I read and watch state and vigilante forms of violence, from James Bond to Jack Reacher, and responses thereto—Montalbano, Rebus, Bosch, Rawlins. I think Samuel Dashiell Hammett and Raymond Thornton Chandler, dealers in the masculine code of controlled violence, and Shakespeare, dealer in bloody historiography, are among the greatest innovators writing in English.

Cultural materialism and discourse

That is probably not an atypical history of failings and tastes. It illustrates the interpersonal, collective, and criminal nature of violence, its complex topography and history, and informs the more academic aspect to this book. Moving across the conceptual and geographical board, I argue for a way of understanding violence that goes beyond supposedly universal human traits to focus on specificities of history, place, and population via cultural materialism, discourse analysis, and case studies. I deploy categorical devices from the social sciences as grids of investigation, but I question their status as machines obliterating difference. I hope this produces an intellectual polyphony that draws out contradictions and dissonances.

Cultural materialism looks at structural determinations on people versus their own agency across time and space. It is animated by subjectivity and power—how human subjects are formed and experience culture and society. The approach takes its agenda and mode of analysis from economics, politics, communication studies, sociology, literature, area studies, education, law, science and technology studies, anthropology, philosophy, media studies, and history, with a particular focus on gender, race, class, and sexuality in everyday life. It commingles textual and social theory under the sign of a commitment to progressive change—a hybrid of critical political economy and cultural studies.

Cultural materialism works with Marx's insight that people manufacture their own conditions of existence, but often without a conscious or enabling agency. Social practices make life and change it over time. This insight directs us away from any view of historical and contemporary culture that privileges aesthetic civilization, the experiences of rulers, or the prelates of religion (Williams, 1977: 19). The result articulates material culture (television, weaponry, assault, and so on) with sociohistorical change (political regimes, economic conjunctures, imperialism, etc.).

This is as per Gramsci's model of hegemony, a process of securing consent to the social order that makes dominant culture appear normal and natural. That order incorporates extant residual cultures, which comprise old meanings and practices that are no longer dominant but remain influential. Emergent cultural practices may be propagated by a new class or co-opted by elites (1971).

That said, I eschew reading off phenomena as reflections of a prevailing mode of production. *Violence* links cultural materialism to Foucault's account of discursive formations, which is often regarded as anti-Marxist. I think that is wrongheaded. The microphysics of power can be equally Marxist and Foucauldian. Foucault was forever critically engaging Sartrean humanistic Marxism and Althusserian structuralist Marxism. It is worth recalling Foucault's recommendation to 'open Althusser's books' (1989:

14) and the latter's contention that 'something from my writings has passed into his' (Althusser, 1969: 256). As Foucault said of their relationship, 'I followed' (1991b: 55).

There is a significant link between Althusser and Foucault in their theorization of subjects, objects, representation, and interpretation. The accusation of functionalist Marxism sometimes leveled at Althusser, because of his totalizing view of ideological and repressive state apparatuses (1977), is similar to certain critics' lament for the absence of an outside to power in Foucault. Of course, there are major methodological differences as well as similarities. Althusser investigated problematics and their underpinning ideology in the context of the real. Conversely, Foucault researched statements in archives—their preconditions and discursive formations. Only Althusser privileged the idea of his knowledge as scientifically derived and inviolable.

Foucault's principal quibbles with Marxism lay in its focus on class, to the comparative exclusion of struggle, and the totalizing certitudes of ideology critique. In particular, he sought to understand material manifestations of power that were not simply used to accrete *bourgeois* dominance or state authority—hence his archival readings of prisons, hospitals, and asyla. These commitments revealed that the micropolitics of forming and controlling subjects were not always and everywhere functions of macroeconomic forces, and had as much to do with dispersing power as accumulating or exercising it (Foucault, 1980: 58, 1982: 782).

Foucault's concept of biopower drew extensively on Marx to construct homologies between civil and military training via 'docile bodies.' Comparing the division of labor to the organization of infantry, *Discipline and Punish* (1977) has many cultural-materialist features in its account of how disciplinary power developed alongside capitalism, as elites addressed the interrelated tasks of developing and maintaining a productive and compliant labor force and social order. One can pick up on these insights to consider postindustrial forms of sociality (Sibilia, 2009).

And in terms of progressive social movements, Foucault's participation and inspiration cannot be doubted. His political actions were often shared with Sartre or inspired by his example, for all that the a priori reasoning subject at the heart of existentialism was foreign to Foucault's projects, like its equivalent in bourgeois Anglo-Yanqui liberalism. Foucault joined the Maoist Gauche Proletarienne (Proletarian Left), helped develop *Gai Pied* (*Gay Foot*), and was a founder of the Groupe d'Information sur les Prisons (Information Group on Prisons). It is also worth noting that his research and public intellection have inspired leftists living under authoritarian regimes, such as the Argentine junta (Friera, 2004). The presumed opposition between Foucault and Marxism also forgets the fundamental anti-imperialism that underpinned much of his work; the 1970s lectures on biopolitics investigated how colonialism gave Europe new life by pauperizing the rest of the world (2003b, 2004).

The book you hold in your hands

Endless debates continue over how to define and count violence, with significant similarities and differences between organizations, countries, epochs, languages, activists, and researchers. They exemplify cultural, intellectual, temporal, and political coalitions and divisions that frequently blur lines and confuse categories—and are rarely used effectively to counter mythology. For example, since 2001 within the United States, twice as many citizens have been murdered by right-wing white men as Islamists (The Peace Alliance, 2015). Global terrorism killed 25,000 people in 2017 (Institute for Economics & Peace, 2017: 2). By way of contrast, *1.34 million worldwide die each year in traffic accidents* (World Health Organization, 2018). Yet we do not see mainstream panic over white men or automobiles.

Violence engages these issues in a wide-ranging interdisciplinary form, examining definitions and data, psychology and ideology, gender, nation-states, and the media. I pose—and provisionally answer—several foundational questions:

- how has violence been defined, historically and geographically?
- has it decreased or increased over time?
- which regions of the world are the most violent?
- does violence correlate with economies, political systems, and religions?
- what is the relationship of gender and violence? and
- what role do the media play?

The book blends synopsis and originality, exploring how numerous disciplines within the human sciences have sought to define, explain, and control violence across time and space.

In writing this volume, I have not forgotten my own complicity with violence, in person and in culture, both when that complicity is collective and historical (an imperial and gendered heritage) and individual (as a participant, reader, and spectator). As mentioned earlier, I also use case studies to illustrate my points, in keeping with the stories that began this introduction.

Such an awareness is neither a passport to understanding nor a frontier marking out the totality of experience. But behind every statistic lie definitions and stories replete with contested truths and contesting parties. I hope the virtue of the book is its preparedness to lay bare some of those differences in a way that privileges theory, fact, fiction, and experience in dynamic interaction.

1 Meaning and data

This first chapter looks at definitions and numbers. Just as the meaning of many abstract nouns is contingent and contested, so is the signifier of 'violence.' As a consequence, there are many controversies over the nature of the topic, quite apart from differences of opinion and practice over how to classify, collect, and respond to the statistics it generates. I endeavor here to outline some of these definitions and associated problems, what might be made of the numbers (albeit under erasure), and how they can elucidate two particular issues: intimate and domestic violence, and violence in the United States.

Whatever 'violence' signifies, and however much of it there is, we probably all agree that its material referents matter—that this is one of the world's most enduring and pressing issues. From time immemorial, violence has been a key theme of religions, societies, families, economies, and politics. It is a central concern of public policy, social movements, academic research, drama, journalism, fiction, war, and policing. Hegel suggested that one could regard 'History as the slaughter bench' of collective suffering and the formation of states (2008: 123). For Joyce, 'History . . . is a nightmare from which I am trying to awake' (2000: 316) and later, a 'nightmare from which you will never awake' (2000: 641).

In other words, violence is a universal problem. Whether we look at nuclear weaponry, cartel rivalry, or domestic assault, it stalks both macro- and micro-discussions of international, social, and interpersonal relations. I cannot imagine news, criminology, health care, so-called social media, or Congress without discussions of violence. For example, no US news organization can resist concluding the old year and ushering in the new one without reviewing annual numbers of homicides, whether locally or nationally (Monkonnen, 2001: 1).

Women around the world must avoid violence on a daily basis, on the street and in the home (World Health Organization, 2013). For working-class US youth, the military is the best bet for ongoing employment (Miller,

2008). Colombians aged under 75 have no experience of life beyond the conflict/civil war that began in the 1940s. Australians date their emergence as a nation from the attempt to invade Turkey in 1915 (McKay, 2018). French and US citizens rise to national anthems celebrating weaponry and slaughter. For religious believers, deities are intimately bound to crime and punishment. And a lock on the legitimate use of force is foundational to the essence of the state and intimately bound up with the nation that legitimizes it via mythic origins and obligations (Weber, 1946).

Violence is generally thought of 'as an event or action that is immediate in time, explosive and spectacular in space . . . erupting into instant sensational visibility' (Nixon, 2011: 2). That is probably the dominant understanding in popular, governmental, and scholarly discourse.

But the term itself undergoes regular and contentious redefinition. There are differences between state, collective, and interpersonal violence, between planned and passional violence, and between fatal and non-fatal forms. Violence is not only physical. Even proponents of absolute free speech worry about hateful words either indexing or provoking violence, whether they arise interpersonally or demagogically. Violence 'can be legal or illegal, visible or invisible, necessary or redundant, illogical or rational and strategic' (Ahluwalia *et al.*, 2007: 1).

People's experiences of violence generate different understandings of it. Low-income, marginal groups in Colombia came up with 60 different definitions in the late 1990s, mostly connected to economic deprivation (Moser and McIlwaine, 2000: 2). Numerous difficult questions arise from such varied discourses. If countries have dual legal systems for indigenous and other citizens, or if religions require adherents to obey separate and incompatible laws, what happens when distinctive notions of criminality and punishment are in conflict within secular nation-states (Black, 2019)? And what do we make of capital cases where defenses are based on cultural relativism? Such arguments have been mobilized, for example, to exonerate a Chinese-American man who murdered his wife, a Japanese-American woman who killed her children (each because of adultery), and a Hmong man who abducted and raped a Laotian-American woman. In each case, the assailants maintained they were acting in accordance with their cultures of origin (Benhabib, 2002: 86–91). And of course, is the death penalty an infringement of human rights (Steiker and Steiker, 2019), and how does it relate to such defenses?

What of violence done to oneself? Some might query discussion of self-harm in this volume, but of course it includes what are controversially known as 'altruistic' suicides, associated with 神風 (*Kamikaze*), حزب الله (Hezbollah), தமிழீழ விடுதலைப் புலிகள் (Liberation Tigers of Tamil Eelam), القاعدة (Al-Qaeda), and assorted suicide-vest wearers and explosives-laden truck drivers. In such instances, the body is transformed into a bomb, whose destruction is a guaranteed and necessary part of harming others. There is a coeval desire to kill and to die and a high degree of ideological commitment and collective organization, rather than anomic individual suffering. Ronald Reagan was cowed by such suicide attacks on US troops in 1980s Lebanon, and he withdrew his occupiers. That reaction encouraged countless attacks in the decades since (Barbagli, 2015: 954–1050).

Then there is the much less personally directed and dramatic, but equally destructive, form: what Robert Nixon calls 'slow violence,' enacted by the dread hand of development, capital, international organizations, and states. This is:

> a violence that occurs gradually and out of sight, a violence of delayed destruction that is dispersed across time and space, an attritional violence that is typically not viewed as violence at all . . . neither spectacular nor instantaneous, but rather incremental and accretive, its calamitous repercussions playing out across a range of temporal scales.
>
> (Nixon, 2011: 2)

That violence is destroying our very Earth.

Given this complexity, I have adopted a nominalist position on the meaning of 'violence,' such that it signifies in a commonsensical way to cover physical harm done to others. But many other aspects come and go with the efflux of time and space, as social movements, laws, and geopolitics create different circumstances and discourses.

The World Health Organization (WHO) favors this broad definition:

> The intentional use of physical force or power, threatened or actual, against oneself, another person, or against a group or community, that either results in or has a high likelihood of resulting in injury, death, psychological harm, maldevelopment or deprivation. It takes the forms of self-directed violence, interpersonal violence and collective violence.
>
> (2002)

That version has been enormously influential in its inclusion of emotion, poverty, and power as well as direct and immediate injury (Lee, 2019: 4).

The Organization for Economic Co-operation and Development (OECD) specifies political violence as:

> the use of force towards a political end that is perpetrated to advance the position of a person or group defined by their political position

in society. Governments, state militaries, rebels, terrorist organisations and militias engage in political violence, as well as actors who may adopt both political and criminal motives.

(2016: 20)

It describes social violence like this:

a broader manifestation of grievances, criminal behaviours and interpersonal violence in society. These include multiple types of crime, homicides, and interpersonal and self-directed violence.

(2016: 20)

Complexities abound. For the last quarter of a century, the United Nations (UN) has approached 'human security' as 'much more than freedom from violence and crime.' In 2012, it adopted a definition that incorporated 'challenges to survival, livelihood and dignity' as obstacles to the desired goal that people should be able to 'exercise choices safely and freely' (Gómez and Gasper, 2013).

These definitions both derive from and inform policies and laws, which vary hugely. For example, at what stage of life are people deemed to be criminally violent and worthy of punishment for their actions? Over 40 countries nominate 14 years of age, a few 16, but the figure is often much lower, especially across the Global South. In South Asia, it is mostly 7 years of age ('If a 13,' 2019). And whose lives matter most? In the United States, data on the slaughter of African Americans and Native Americans were less complete than those covering deaths of European Americans (Roth, 2009: xii).

Consider when and where statistical history 'begins.' Numerical data on violence are notoriously difficult to follow or have faith in, given wide differences in the definition and collection of information across time and space (OECD, 2016). Has Colombia been in a civil war for 70 years? And if so, did it end with the 2016 peace accord between two of the principal parties (Miller, 2020)? And how might one compare the data with the level of killing in Latin America prior to and during the Spanish and Portuguese conquest and subsequent struggles for independence? Is the Korean War still in play, given that no peace treaty has been concluded since the horror of the 1950s, when four million died (Cumings 2010: 35)? Does the incarceration of so many African Americans represent a continuity with the violence of the slave trade and hence should be counted as such (Davis, 2003)? If a woman kills an abusive partner, does that constitute murder, manslaughter, or neither (Belew, 2010)? Why did knife crime among the young suddenly become so prevalent in 21st-century London, across racial and class divisions, and what is the basis for comparing it with the previous decade (A New Approach, 2018)?

How should one adjudicate between the numbers presented by the military, the police, the judiciary, hospitals, and non-government organizations on supposedly similar topics? The UN Office on Drugs and Crime claims that its coverage of violent crime now extends to three-quarters of the world's population and over half of all countries (2017). But controversy abounds whenever serious attempts are made to meet the UN Population Fund's call for adequate data on 'the nature and magnitude' of violence against women, not least because gendered assault 'is sensitive and often hidden.' Police and medical reports 'represent the tip of the iceberg' and coordinated efforts to compile comparable data internationally only date from this century (2013). Over the past decade, the Gender Equality Observatory for Latin America and the Caribbean has developed a 'regional femicide indicator.' It shows that almost 4,000 women in the area's 34 nations were murdered in gendered ways in 2018—a number that is rather dubious, as many countries only count partner killings, or exclude them (2019).

And executions? Almost 150 countries do not have or apply the death penalty, but it is used with seeming relish in others. Whereas 1,634 people were executed in 2015, the number had fallen to fewer than a thousand a year later. Religious states were the keenest: Iran, Saudi Arabia, Pakistan, and Iraq accounted for 84%. But because the preternaturally frightened Chinese state considers such assassinations to be state secrets, no one outside its anxious administrative cloisters knows those numbers (Amnesty International, 2018).

The Pentagon declined to account for civilian deaths in Panamá in 1989, or Yugoslavia ten years later (Herman, 2004: 6–7). When asked if he knew how many Iraqis had died as a result of the 1991 conflict, Chairman of the Joint Chiefs of Staff Colin Powell replied, 'It's really not a number I'm terribly interested in' (quoted in Zinn, 2003: x); and Secretary of State Madeleine Albright announced in 1996 that although the death of half a million Iraqi children because of economic sanctions 'was a very hard choice . . . we think the price is worth it' (quoted in Roy, 2002: 225).

When the *Lancet*, one of the world's major medical journals, published an epidemiological paper late in 2004 suggesting that 100,000 people may have died from violence in Iraq since DC and its allied lapdogs invaded the year before, the US media barely noted the fact, despite the story's prominence elsewhere. Three months later, the nation's TV networks began to discuss the number of Iraqi dead, with their 'estimates' ranging between 16,500 and 20,000. Reporters discredited the *Lancet* study, despite support for it among mortality and bio-statistical experts (Roberts *et al.*, 2004; FAIR, 2005). It ran counter to the bourgeois media's faithful reportage of

Pentagon data, which had been *in*flated during the American War in Việt Nam, in order to pretend the military was winning; *de*flated thereafter to pretend they were humane; then redeployed to claim success in murdering non-state terrorists while suppressing word of civilian casualties (Richardson, 2017).

México's homicide level briefly crested in 2017 at 25% greater than the previous record high (Institute for Economics & Peace, 2018: 2). Then there were 28,839 homicides in 2018, up 15% on 2017 (Martínez, 2019). By July 2019, someone was murdered every 15 minutes (Observatorio Nacional, 2019). As the Covid-19 virus hit, March 2020 became the deadliest month on record, with over 2,500 homicides (Ferri, 2020). These horrendous numbers were fueled by a weak but violent state and a noxious blend of needy nostrils in the Global North matched by craven criminalization south of the border. The Consejo Ciudadano Para La Seguridad Pública y La Justicia Penal AC (Citizens' Council for Public Safety and Penal Justice) placed five Mexican cities in the top ten of its 50 most violent urban regions in the world for 2018; the others were in Venezuela and Brazil (2019).

The numbers, under erasure

With all those caveats in place, where possible I use statistics with strong inter-agency, inter-authorial correlations. In terms of what appear to be relatively independent and rigorous 21st-century accounts, well over 1.5 million people worldwide die each year from violence. It is one of the biggest causes of death for teenagers up to people in their mid-forties (The Peace Alliance, 2015). Excluding wars, interpersonal violence is the 19th largest cause of mortality around the world, at over 400,000 deaths a year. It is also responsible for substantial morbidity as an aftereffect for victims and those close to them (Fazel *et al.*, 2018).

Of the roughly 250,000 people killed by firearms worldwide in 2016, half perished in the Americas and the Caribbean, which host around 8% of the world's population. Europe and Oceania are the safest places to be (Global Burden of Disease, 2016 Injury Collaborators, 2018; OECD, 2016).[1] Of course, South America shows very significant statistical variations in terms of the level of homicide. The northern part, notably Brazil, Colombia, and Venezuela, has higher rates than the southern cone, and the highest in the world after Southern Africa and Central America. Colombia now averages 30.8 murders per 100,000 people, whereas the figure is 7.9 for Uruguay and 3.1 for Chile. Historical variation also plays its part: the number of killings in Colombia was greatest during the fever pitch of its conflict—the 1950s and 1990s. The violence decreased with the introduction of limited hours of alcohol availability but was spurred on again by contests over cocaine production and distribution (United Nations Office on Drugs and Crime, 2014: 22–23, 26, 37, 75–76). Even as global conflicts involving sovereign states increase the numbers of refugees and fatalities, over 80% of violent deaths occur through social assaults (OECD, 2016).

Recent Pollyannaish analysts argue that war is, so to speak, dying out. They appear to rely on the Uppsala Conflict Data Program, which requires state participation and battlefield casualties for violent events to be counted (Kaldor, 2012: 10–11). But numerous non-state collective actors engage in armed struggle, defined as 'conflict between two organized groups which results in at least 25 annual battle-related deaths' (Sundberg *et al.*, 2012). That trend has increased since the end of the Cold War: there were 20 such instances in 1989, 40 in 2000, and over 80 in 2018. Almost 19,000 people perished on 2018's battlefields, the majority in Arabic and sub-Saharan Africa plus México. Over 100,000 die annually in non-state struggles (Melander *et al.*, 2016; Rudolfsen, 2019).

For many years, the Institute for Economics and Peace has produced a quantoid and qualtoid Global Peace Index (GPI). It argues that since 2008:

> Global peacefulness has deteriorated by 3.78 per cent, with 81 GPI countries recording a deterioration, and 81 improving, highlighting that deteriorations in peacefulness are generally larger than improvements. The index has deteriorated for eight of the last twelve years, with the last improvement in peacefulness before 2019 occurring in 2014.
>
> (Institute for Economics & Peace, 2019: 2)

Relatively peaceful countries, such as Iceland, report higher levels of personal security and faith in governments and police forces (Institute for Economics & Peace, 2019: 2–3). Conversely, a fifth of Mexicans say they have suffered violence at the hands of the police and a quarter experience homicides in their lives (Instituto Nacional de Estadística y Geografía, 2018).

More environmental defenders have been killed over the last decade and a half than British and Australian soldiers fighting in US wars. The places where these activists are assassinated grow in number annually—683 people died worldwide in 2017, over a third of them resisting agribusiness and minerals extraction (Butt *et al.*, 2019). Many more were tossed into jail or threatened. All had dared to question rapacious land use by the extractive industries. They became victims of a vicious amalgam of the state, contract assassins, and private security forces (Global Witness, 2019).

Intimate/domestic violence

The United Nations defines violence against women as

> any act of gender-based violence that results in, or is likely to result in, physical, sexual, or mental harm or suffering to women, including threats of such acts, coercion or arbitrary deprivation of liberty, whether occurring in public or in private life.
>
> (1993)

The US National Coalition Against Domestic Violence describes it as 'the willful intimidation, physical assault, battery, sexual assault, and/or other abusive behavior as part of a systematic pattern of power and control perpetrated by one intimate partner against another. It includes physical violence, sexual violence, threats, and emotional/psychological abuse' and notes that 'frequency and severity . . . varies dramatically' (2019).

The WHO (2017) estimates that a third of women across the world have been assaulted by lovers or strangers, to the point where this must be considered a core 'global health problem' (2013: 1). The proportion is lowest—less than a quarter—in the Global North. Well over a third of murdered women are killed by partners. The pattern is of male assailants and female victims who share low educational levels, mistreatment when young, histories of their mothers being battered, alcohol problems, and a claim or fear of male superiority and entitlement, plus lack of female financial autonomy. Apart from death, outcomes for women include disease, pregnancy, infertility, alcoholism, tobacco use, and depression.

In 2017, US men murdered almost 2,000 women 'in single victim/single offender incidents.' Over 90% of them killed women they knew, and more than 60% were sexual partners (Violence Policy Center, 2019a). Most female rape victims (90%) are assaulted by people they know/are involved with romantically. One in 71 men and 1 in 5 women experience rape; 1 in 6 men and 1 in 3 women some form of sexual violence. The numbers for indigenous women amount to almost half that population (National Sexual Violence Resource Center, 2019).

Every minute, 20 people experience domestic violence in the US—over ten million each year, which constitutes 15% of the nation's violent crime. A third of women and a quarter of men have experienced physical violence at the hands of an intimate partner. A tenth of women have been raped by their 'lovers,' making up 20% of rape victims. Around 20,000 calls are made to emergency service phone numbers dedicated to the problem. Young women aged 18 to 24 are the likeliest sufferers. A third of female homicides are perpetrated by partners, and a fifth of male ones (National Coalition Against Domestic Violence, 2019).

Almost two-thirds of UK women aged between 18 and 39 have been unwillingly slapped or bitten by men during otherwise consensual sex, two-thirds have had their hair pulled, more than a third have been choked or gagged, and a fifth spat on (Savanta ComRes, 2019). London's underground mass transit service saw a 40% increase in sex attacks from 2014 to 2018 ('PA Media,' 2019). Between 2000 and 2018, 126 people in Wales and England lost their lives to terrorism; the corollary number for people murdered by family members/lovers was 1,870 (Doward, 2019).

In Australia, which has a population of around 25 million, there were 152 intimate-partner homicides between 2010 and 2014, 80% of which saw men killing women as the culmination of a pattern of violence. Most remaining murders were of men killed by women whom they had long abused. Alcohol was a factor in half the killings of women. Indigenous male and female assailants were over-represented demographically (Australian Domestic and Family Violence Death Review Network, 2018). Of people over the age of 15, 1 in 6 women and 1 in 16 men have been victims of violence perpetrated by current or former partners. One in 5 women and 1 in 20 men have been sexually threatened or assaulted (Australian Institute of Health and Warfare, 2018). The Australian Human Rights Commission notes that female victims of domestic violence have high levels of associated illness, notably mental-health suffering; feminist human-rights defenders experience numerous threats online; and indigenous women are three times as likely to be victims of violence or threats as others (2017).

New Zealand/Aotearoa has a population of well under five million people. Between 2014 and 2018, almost 24,000 sex crimes were reported to the police, nearly two-thirds of them against children. Six percent of the alleged perpetrators served time. The Red Chilena Contra La Violencia Hacia Las Mujeres (Chilean Network Against Violence Towards Women) (2018–19) estimates the nation of 19 million had 32 femicides in the first semester of 2019, eight more than the official figure; over the last decade, the Red generally listed between 50 and 60 femicides annually, against the state's 40 (Ministry of Justice, 2019).

The United States

The United States deserves its own sub-heading in virtually every category of violence. The Bureau of Justice Statistics (BJS) found that victims of violence aged over 12 grew from 2.7 million in 2015 to 3.1 million in 2017, more than double the cases reported to the police (Morgan and Truman, 2018). This is the only advanced industrial society with rampant killing; one of the few democracies to sanction the death penalty; and a cavalier attitude to gun ownership.

When the Civil War ended, Union and Confederate troops were allowed to take their guns with them: the fons et origo of today's culture of owning weapons. The National Rifle Association (NRA) was founded soon after (Densley and Peterson, 2017: 9). Initially a rather mild-mannered, Clark-Kentish advocate for field sports, a hostile takeover in the 1970s saw it depart Gotham for the wilds and begin arguing that the Second Amendment to the Constitution guarantees the right to carry arms in self-defense (Densley and Peterson, 2017: 11). The amendment actually provides that 'a well-regulated militia, being necessary to the security of a free State, the right of the people to keep and bear arms, shall not be infringed.' The Association has become a major political player (see Figure 1.1). It ensures that the conditions of existence for violence are maintained and developed, to the point where 'mass shootings in America have become like deforestation in Brazil or air pollution in China—a man-made environmental hazard that is hard to stop' ('America Is the Only,' 2019).

The direction taken by the NRA relates to the transformation of both major political parties since the 1960s. The Democrats have transcended their earlier alliance of rural segregationist Southerners and industrial Northerners into a new grouping of the culture industries, urban professionals, secularists, minorities, and immigrants. The Republicans have transmogrified from an alliance of manufacturing capital and suburbanites into one formed of evangelical Protestants, rural workers, investors, and military families.

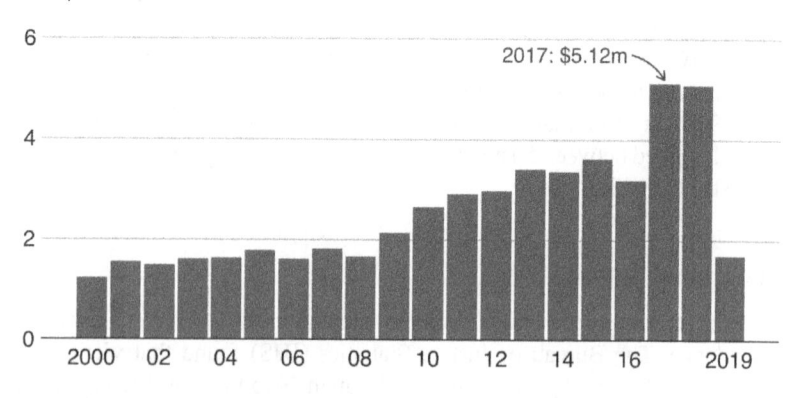

Note: 2019 figures January to July

Figure 1.1 Annual spending on lobbying by National Rifle Association
Source: Center for Responsive Politics

The United States has higher levels of gun ownership than any other country, courtesy of this dedicated and partisan political bloc and evangelicals militating for ownership of machines designed to maim and kill. Almost a third of US residents exercise this putative right (Densley and Peterson, 2017).

Gun suicides and homicides account for more deaths every six months than US citizens killed on September 11, 2001, and in the subsequent wars in Afghanistan and Iraq. In the first two decades of the 21st century, over half a million people in the United States died at the hand of firearms, with the numbers escalating over time to more than 40,000 a year.[2] Almost half a million people were attacked with guns in 2017 (Morgan and Truman, 2018). In 2019, mass killings (i.e., those with at least four people murdered) surpassed previous records: 211 lives taken in 41 incidents (Helmore, 2019).

US homicide rates are seven times the norm of the Global North in general, and killings by firearm 25.2 times higher:

> The next most homicidal affluent democracy, Canada, has had only a quarter of the homicides per capita . . . since World War II . . . others have had from a fifth of the U.S. number per capita (Australia) to less than a tenth (Ireland).
>
> (Roth, 2009: 4)

Crime in general is not a bigger problem in the US than other OECD countries, but firearm ownership and its fatal use are staggeringly greater (Grinshteyn and Hemenway, 2016). Where people live is relevant, with Missouri by far the deadliest state. Close readings of the statistics on black homicide victims disclose a rate of over 20 per 100,000 people, versus an overall national rate of 5 per 100,000; when controlled for gender, black men were victims at a rate of 37 per 100,000, nearly all through use of firearms (Violence Policy Center, 2019b). While race and age are germane (it's best to be Asian and/or over 65), the clearest correlation is between income and safety: 50 of every 1,000 people with household incomes below $10,000 were victims in 2017, just 15 of whom had more than $75,000 in earnings (Morgan and Truman, 2018).

The BBC has generated the useful charts in Figures 1.2–1.4, demonstrating the dimensions/*dementia.*

Propagandized by spectacular instances of mass murder, the US public is largely unaware that violent crime has been decreasing over the last quarter of a century, and hence it leaves itself open to law-and-order thunder (Gramlich, 2019; Blair and Schweit, 2014). It is no surprise, then, that the annual price paid to sustain the violence containment industry—police, the judiciary, and prisons—was at least USD 2.16 trillion in 2015, or 15% of gross domestic product (The Peace Alliance, 2015). The annual cost to

Figure 1.2 An international comparison of gun-related killings as a percentage of all homicides

Source: FBI, Homicide Index Home Office, Statistics Canada, Australia Crime Statistics

Victims killed

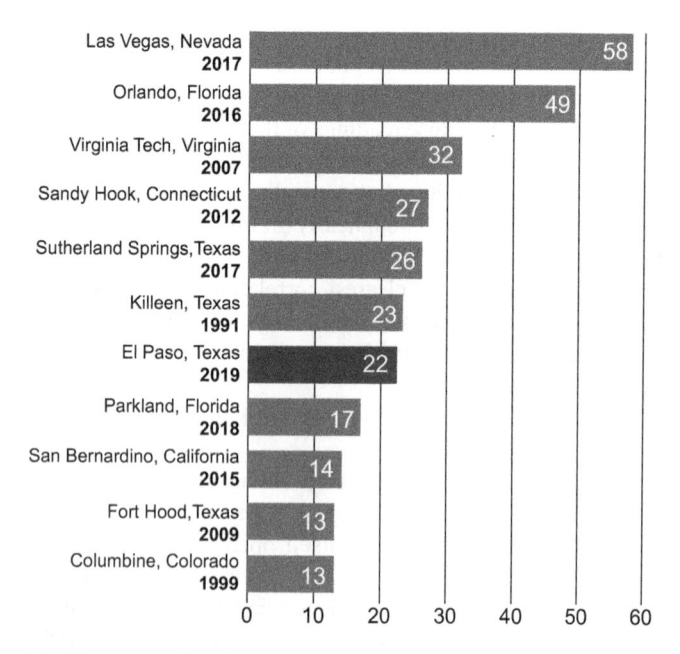

Figure 1.3 Worst mass shootings in the US since 1991

Source: FBI/Las Vegas Police

Firearms per 100 residents

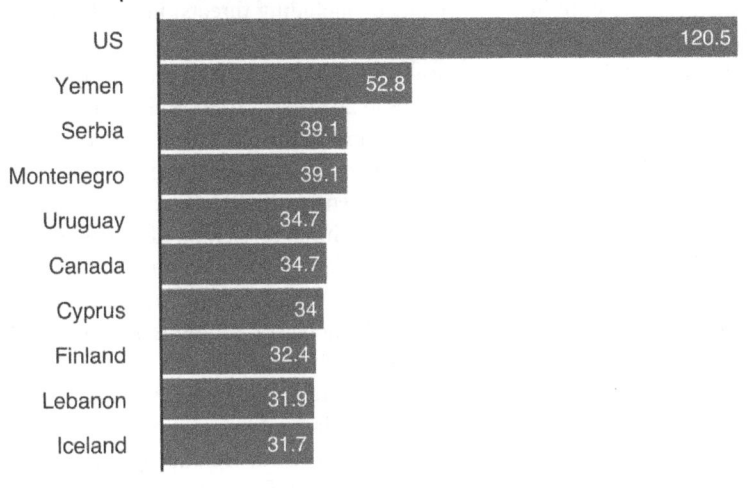

Figure 1.4 Top ten civilian gun-owning countries
Source: Small Arms Survey 2018

productivity from violent crime is almost USD 3 billion (National Sexual Violence Resource Center, 2019).

Measures enacted to deal with firearm murder target the mentally ill, most of whom are not violent. Much-vaunted background checks of gun buyers that invade their medical privacy are of dubious value. And in any event, almost half of US gun sales are undertaken in the secondhand world, often eluding federal oversight (Densley and Peterson, 2017). Data on murder-suicides are still not collected systematically, but the perpetrators are generally men against their families. The best estimates suggest 11 cases a week (Violence Policy Center, 2018).

Profiles of mass shooters across half a century disclose certain characteristics in common: trauma and experience of violence when young; a crisis coinciding with the crime; an interest in other such killers and their motives (hence the tendency towards clusters of killing); and availability of firearms, frequently within families (Peterson and Densley, 2019).

There is a great deal of drama surrounding US school shootings and the horror of children killed and wounded. The rate of youth homicide is 11 per 100,000, by contrast with 0.4 in Japan, 0.6 in France, 0.8 in Germany, and 0.9 in Britain (The Peace Alliance, 2015).[3] Very few Yanqui youth homicides occur at school (around 2.6%), although 2014 saw almost half a million violent acts in middle and high schools. They were generally associated with legal and illegal drug use, family problems, low grades, and poverty (Centers for Disease Control, 2016). Over three-quarters of US K–12 teachers experience bullying, with violence including threats, intimidation, and physical assaults (McMahon *et al.*, 2017).

The informal-sector taxi service Uber admits to 6,000 sexual assaults by its drivers and passengers across the US in 2017–18 (2019). Being a US college student makes one a prime target for rape—about a quarter of female and a sixth of male students are coerced into sex, and two-thirds report harassment (National Sexual Violence Resource Center, 2019). Their suffering does not end with physical recovery; for two-thirds of victims of violence in the United States, 'socio-emotional problems' develop and continue for a month or more. This is especially true for women (Langton and Truman, 2014).

Hate crimes are assaults on sexual, racial, or religious identities. The desire is to humiliate those immediately affected and terrorize both them and those in similar social and cultural categories. Racial issues are easily the biggest focus in the United States, followed by religion and sexuality (Marzullo and Libman, 2009). When the Federal Bureau of Investigation advises that 2017 saw '7,175 hate crime incidents' in the United States, how does that relate to slavery and contemporary white supremacists, when almost half the 2017 'single-bias hate crime offenses' were committed against African Americans? How does it connect to historic anti-Semitism, given that around 60% of 'religious-biased offenses' were against Jewish folks (U. S. Department of Justice, 2018)? And how does the number of incidents synchronize with the annual average of 250,000 hate-crime victimizations between 2004 and 2015 declared by the BJS, which draws on surveys to go beyond police cases (Masucci and Langton, 2017)?

Although the United States offers a mountain of statistics about violence emanating from the official and third sectors, there is one glaring absence: police violence. Whereas data on officers killed while on duty are assiduously collected, the same cannot be said when they kill others. National figures are useless, and local statistics are spotty. Social movements and scholars have painted a shocking picture of an average of 1,000 deaths a year, far above the corollary numbers in other parts of the Global North—and the victims are disproportionately minorities ('A Measure,' 2019):

> African American men and women, American Indian/Alaska Native men and women, and Latino men face higher lifetime risk of being killed by police than do their white peers. . . . Latina women and Asian/ Pacific Islander men and women face lower risk of being killed by police than do their white peers. Risk is highest for black men, who (at current levels of risk) face about a 1 in 1,000 chance of being killed by police over the life course.
>
> (Edwards *et al.*, 2019)

Conclusion

There are difficulties and differences over how, when, where, and by whom violence is defined and its data collected, classified, promulgated, and acted upon. The numbers are chilling when taken at face value, but more so when we realize that so much official information is regarded as understating the truth.

As I reviewed the extant literature, I was struck by the failure of social and cultural thinkers to look at what psychologists, criminologists, international organizations, and economists had to say on the topic—and vice versa. What follows endeavors to host such dialogs. As we shall see, such fundamental influences as religion, gender, and the state are frequently misrepresented or ignored by government, academia, and the bourgeois media.

Notes

1 I write this as a resident of Latin America who lived in the United States for over 20 years.
2 https://wonder.cdc.gov/controller/datarequest/D76.
3 The Naval Postgraduate School's Center for Homeland Defense and Security maintains excellent visualizations of the history and geography of Yanqui school shootings: www.chds.us/ssdb/incidents-united-states-1970-present/.

2 Mind

Reflecting on his early life of crime, Augustine focused on pleasure—not from the succulent fruit he had seized but the very act of breaking the law: 'criminality was the piquant source.' He discerned three causes of his own violence—a corrupted mind driven by 'insolence,' perverse carnality, and propaganda—and additional ones in others: revenge, theft, fear, envy, and sadism. They all demonstrated a 'lust for domination' (1998: 183–84, 306–07, 232–33). Two things lurked beneath these explanations: class distinctions and religious salvation. He is not alone in these prejudicial fantasies.

Locke denounced 'the perverting influence of customs, the frivolity of opinions, the allurements of pleasures, the violence of passions and the enthusiasm of parties.' They 'confuse and mislead our feeble minds in such diverse ways' (1997: 75). In his notorious critique of the popular, Ortega y Gasset argued that 'the element of terror in the destiny of our time is furnished by the overwhelming and violent moral upheaval of the masses; imposing, invincible, and treacherous' (1930: 12).

Milton regarded a newfound atheism among priests as a particular offense because it flooded 'the house of God' with 'lust and violence' (2005: 31). Voltaire reflected on the blood he had seen shed through vengeance and ambition and declared 'man is very much like the Devil' (2000: 118). For Hegel, this represented Christianity's core governing precepts: 'man's becoming conscious that he is evil' but also that 'the good Spirit dwells in him' (2001: 443).

Certainty in one's own ultimate superiority as revealed and nurtured by religion works well with the drive to corral or exterminate the other. In the wake of September 11, 2001, Republican intellectual Ann Coulter called on the government to identify where terrorists lived, 'invade their countries, kill their leaders and convert them to Christianity' (*National Review* Online, October 13, 2001).

Discussions of violence inevitably lead to a focus on just such motivations and drives—the links between what people think, believe, and feel and their physical conduct towards others. Perhaps most popularly among these discourses, psychology seeks to establish whether violence is an essential or malleable human trait, leading to debates about evolutionary social psychology and natural versus nurturing forces. This second chapter looks at understandings of humanness in psychology and criminology, the issues of suicide and sports, and the relationships between religion, ideology, and violence.

The psy-function and criminology

Foucault explains that:

> The fundamental role of the psychological function, which historically is entirely derived from the dissemination of psychiatric power in other directions beyond the asylum, is to intensify reality as power and to intensify power by asserting it as reality.
>
> (2006: 190)

The psy-function plays a crucial part in biopolitics. The *New Scientist* maintains that 'the human condition is now so thoroughly medicalized that few people can claim to be normal' (quoted in Hansen *et al.*, 2003: 12).

The human sciences have been scarred (and are scarring) because of their insistent prognostications about criminal tendencies, particularly towards violence. True believers in the biological roots of conduct are even prominent in the pop-psychology US trade-book market. Steven Pinker announces a 'retreat from violence' in what 'may be . . . the most peaceable era in our species' existence.' The basic line is that everyone has both conflictual and cooperative, violent and peaceful aspects to their cognition and affect, which are tempered by prevailing sociocultural milieux. Massive variations of violence over time and space, or persistent violence, find these essentialists throwing their hands in the air (Raine, 2013: 125). They refer to the 'decivilizing' antics of 'gangs of drugged or drunken hooligans'—the bizarre explanation for Colombia's two centuries of conflict (Pinker, 2011: 437). What is the history of the psy-function's hegemony in debates about violence?

Throughout the 19th century, psychiatry intervened in the legal field of the Global North, establishing its right to define individuals as sane or otherwise, and claiming a role in justice and punishment. Penal law codified 'dangerous individuals' as monomaniacal, degenerate, perverse, constitutionally unbalanced, and immature (Foucault, 2000). A century ago, George Still, Britain's first chair of child medicine, was 'collecting observations . . . of defective moral control as a morbid condition . . . in association with idiocy or imbecility.' He famously discerned an inherited neurological disorder that produced 'defects of inhibitory volition,' purportedly leading to an 'abnormal defect of moral control' via theft, sex, violence, mendacity, and hyperactivity (1902). This was a pioneering moment in the association of mental illness/disability with violence, followed by decade after decade of psychiatrists, clinical psychologists, and their kind seeking such causal links:

> The traditional view (among those who come from cultures that emphasize individualism) is to look within for answers—for pathology or heroism. Modern psychiatry is dispositionally oriented. So are clinical psychology and personality and assessment psychology. Most of our institutions are founded on such a perspective, including law, medicine, and religion. Culpability, illness, and sin, they assume, are to be found within the guilty party, the sick person, and the sinner.
>
> (Zimbardo, 2007: 35)

Correlations drawn between crime, poverty, intellect, desire, education, racial formation, and so on have driven much of this work, resulting in a multitude of cruel and useless governmental punishments and popular shibboleths. Epistemologies and methods have been deeply partisan and politicized, producing equivalently partisan and politicized policies and programs. Criminologists, particularly cultural-critical ones, are more prone to emphasize socioeconomic circumstances, state violence, and racialized legal frameworks and implementation (Hawkins, 2003).

Here's the reality: for those suffering severe mental illness and incarcerated in mental wards and hospitals, rates of involvement in violence are significantly higher (17%–50%) than is the case for outpatients (2%–13%). Many of these folks have been victims of violence, which may cause or result from their illnesses. There are more victims than perpetrators (Carpiniello *et al.*, 2020: 4, 6; Fazel *et al.*, 2018). Such attitudes purportedly proliferate in the Global South, born of a history of intense colonial malevolence. That is said to contrast distinctly with the Global North (Puig Abril and Rojas, 2018). Comparative social psychology tends to elude the essentialism of methodological nationalists, who effortlessly extrapolate from local populations. It proposes that authoritarian conservative ideology frequently admires violence when associated with success (Espinosa Pezzia *et al.*, 2017).

Unlike their orthodox colleagues, critical 'social psychologists ask: To what extent can an individual's actions be traced to factors outside the actor, to situational variables and environmental processes unique to a given setting?' (Zimbardo, 2007: 36). Hence Albert Bandura's inquiries into what he termed 'moral disengagement'—the capacity to double-declutch between one's belief about violence and one's violent actions, an ability driven by justifications for contradictory commitments and practices (2016).

Attempts to predict individually violent conduct based on psychological evaluations have proven intensely controversial, their seemingly scientific certitudes often amounting to little more than clairvoyance gilded with professionalism. Three decades ago, the American Psychiatric Association condemned attempts to use this 'expertise' in courts. It estimated that such predictions were wrong two-thirds of the time, rendering them equivalent to guesswork. This was an unacceptable ratio on which to base legal decisions. The Supreme Court disagreed, and the US judiciary continues to take such testimony seriously. As a consequence, the psy-function has dedicated many resources to soothsaying via assessments of risk, without great success. Similar difficulties attend efforts by actuaries to correlate past and future violence, though these methods have proven more accurate than clinical ones. Combining the two is the current gold standard (Scurich, 2016).

The difficulty relates to a paradox identified by Schutz. In trying to understand why a murderer sought 'to achieve his goals by violence rather than by honest labor,' two motives are often sought. The law looks for an 'in-order-to motive,' which 'explains the act in terms of the project.' Conversely, the psy-function goes looking for the 'because-motive.' It 'explains the project in terms of the actor's past experiences' (1972: 91). This is akin to Foucault's tracing of a complex crossroads: the meeting of 'the medical demonstration that insanity is ultimately always dangerous, and of the court's inability to determine the punishment of a crime without having determined the motives for the crime' (1978b: 10). The lack of an easy junction articulating the two tendencies causes problems. It is very telling in the case of suicide.

Suicide

Suicide is widely considered to be improper; it used to be illegal in many countries, and runs counter to a wide variety of religious teachings, including those that privilege martyrdom. Plato had particular contempt for those who took their 'fate out of the hands of destiny' (1997: 4409). Perhaps this is because, in Lotman's words, suicide 'represents a special form of victory over death, of overcoming it,' and is therefore 'contradictory to the natural . . . order of things' (2004: 163), or what Hume called 'that species of Death which they proposed to themselves' (1996: 5). But Hume defended suicide as no more contrary to some deity's will than seeking to stay alive by avoiding a falling rock: each was about taking life into one's own hands in contest with natural occurrences (1996: 6).

More importantly than such philosophical and theistic neuroses, suicide is among the 15 leading global causes of death, and in the top ten for US residents aged 10 to 54 (Swanson *et al.*, 2015). Suicide there is racialized—data from California put the rates per 100,000 at 20 for Native Americans; 18 for whites; seven for African Americas and Asians/Pacific Islanders; and six for Latin@s (Violence Policy Center, 2019c). Worldwide, it's responsible for almost half the violent deaths of people aged between 15 and 44 (Carpiniello *et al.*, 2020: 3). But what causes it?

There are numerous psychological correlates, such as anomie, depression, psychosis, loneliness, failure, drug addiction, gambling, dishonor, and terminal illness. Over the last few years, we have seen significant press coverage of people killing themselves rather than continue working and living in Chinese electronics factories (Fullerton, 2018). When Johann Wolfgang von Goethe's novel *Die Leiden des jungen Werthers* (*The Sorrows of Young Man Werther*) (2013) was released in 1774, its suiciding hero was deemed to have caused numerous copycat suicides among readers. The book was subsequently banned in many cities and gave its name to an epidemiological sub-field, while in the month after Marilyn Monroe's death in 1962, mimetic suicides went up 12% across the United States. That provided what has become a classic case study in the epidemiology of how news coverage of the death of stars can affect the public (Stack, 2003). We see such mimesis in Japan and Korea, where numerous citizens follow the example of suiciding politicians and celebrities immediately after their deaths (Ueda *et al.*, 2014; Lee, 2020). In addition, Twitter updates on mental health coincide with increased suicide (Jashinsky *et al.*, 2014).

Standing on a railway platform awaiting a train one chilly 2014 night, I saw a teenager on the bridge above; ashen-faced and shivering, she was clearly preparing to jump. I ran to the station manager to get him to stop the trains. He refused, saying what happened on the bridge above was outside his jurisdiction. I sped back to a spot below her and said: 'Sweetheart, I don't know what's troubling you, but I can say this: life changes, and you have much of it to experience.' Then I saw a pair of muscular arms enwrap her from behind, in what I took to be a friendly and secure gesture.

The experience jolted me back three decades to my time as a phone-service volunteer working with people contemplating suicide, along with visits to people who had started the process but then wanted to be saved from it. It was something I did weekly for the first half of my twenties. During that period, I struggled with the phone service's (principal, but not exclusionary) Christian and psy-function orientation. I also wanted to downplay the humanistic, non-directive, client-centered approach that it favored. I could see the utility of this method in terms of understanding people in crisis and seeking not to worsen matters for them, as per Rogerian psychotherapy, the most-cited form after Freudianism across the 20th century (Rogers, 1995; Haggbloom *et al.*, 2002): 'You sound upset' worked better than 'Come off it.' But I doubted its efficacy in terms of understanding external (socioeconomic and cultural) aspects of suicide. In those days, few of us thought about the political motivations that could underpin it, as discussed in the introduction.

It appears that the natural rhythms of weather have an impact on self-harm: summer is the season where most suicides occur, along with moments when the temperature rises in an extreme fashion. But what happens with profound climate change? There has been considerable speculation about connections between mental health and global warming, but so far, there has not been a great deal of empirical investigation, though temperature variation correlates strongly with conflict more generally (Hsiang *et al.*, 2013).

Recent research does tie suicide rates to climate change. Consider *Nature*'s comparison of suicide rates in México and the United States (Burke *et al.*, 2018). It examined those two countries for a number of reasons. Between them, they account for about 7% of the world's suicides. Beyond that, they provide information about temperature and suicide over many decades and municipalities. There are lots of factors not directly affiliated with climate, such as the onset or increase in poverty or gun ownership, but which are easily compared independent variables. In addition to suicide statistics, the research sought correlations between social-media expressions of sadness and desperation with temperature change. The results indicate a stronger tendency towards suicide with increased warmth, and vice versa. The rates keep increasing as new temperature records are set. There could be 26,000 suicides in the United States each year by 2050 (Burke *et al.*, 2018).

There are clear similarities between the United States and México, but there are also profound social, cultural, and economic differences. Octavio Paz famously mused on the profound solitude of being Mexican and the dramatic switching points it generates between quietude and violence, politeness and loathing:

> Our sense of inferiority—real or imagined—might be explained at least partly by the reserve with which the Mexican faces other people and the unpredictable violence with which his repressed emotions break through his mask of impassivity.
>
> (1961: 19)

That attitude derives from discomforting racial, class, and linguistic encounters with the United States and in México itself: 'the unforeseen violence that lacerates us, . . . the solemn or convulsive splendor of our fiestas, . . .

our cult of death' (1961: 65). Are there salves that can provide release from such feelings?

Sports

Psychological research connects with sociology in a collective, restless search for outlets to redirect purportedly natural violent tendencies towards codified and controlled physical outlets (e.g., sports). They began in two ways: on the one hand, as unregulated, unruly peasant and proletarian joy, relaxation, and violence (in the street); and on the other, as state and popular pleasure derived from more ordered, if similarly violent, activities (in the Coliseum). They expanded by blending these two forms and mixing volunteer and waged labor, amateur and professional management.

The idea of a dialectical struggle between violence and order, pleasure and passivity underpinning sports and their spectators goes back centuries (Weber, 1992: 112):

> Where violent conflict changes to 'competition,' whether for Olympic wreaths . . . or for social honor or gain . . . regulations serve as 'rules of the game' determining the forms of conflict. . . . The gradually increasing 'pacification,' in the sense of the reduction in the use of physical force, only reduces but does not ever wholly eliminate the appeal to the use of force . . . [which] has been increasingly monopolized by the coercive apparatus of a certain kind of association.
>
> (Weber, 1981: 173)

Elias discerned a largely agreeable sublimation and civilization of dangerous drives—a sanctioned release from the travails of life:

> Battle lust and aggressiveness . . . find socially permitted expression . . . in competitive sports. And they are manifest above all in 'spectating' . . . the daydream-like identification with some few people who, in a moderate and precisely regulated way, are allowed to act out such affects . . . active, pleasurable aggression is transformed into a more passive and restrained pleasure.
>
> (1978: 240)

He investigated the advent of rule-governed contests between individuals and teams, a trend that fanned out from the European ruling classes after the 16th century. Sentiment and behavior became governed, supplanting excess and self-laceration with an almost studious auto-critique. The displacement of tension and the search for ordered leisure allocated to organized sports the task of controlling and training gentry, workers, and colonists alike. High tension and low risk blended popular appeal with public safety in a utilitarian calculus of time and joy. Football (soccer), for example, evolved from the British middle class pacifying, adopting, and codifying unruly male working-class pastimes. It spread across the world during the 19th century in close concert with the UK's colonial, maritime, military, and commercial interests (Elias and Dunning, 1986; Krauze, 1994).

Domestically, this was connected to the 'emergence of the health and physical well-being of the population in general as one of the essential objectives of political power.' The entire 'social body' was assayed and treated for its insufficiencies. Governing people meant, most centrally and critically, obeying the 'imperative of health: at once the duty of each and the objective of all' (Foucault, 2003b: 241).

The 19th-century British inspector of schools, poet, and critic Matthew Arnold looked on, bemused but resigned, as the Industrial Revolution created 'games and sports which occupy the passing generation of boys and young men' in search of 'a better and sounder physical type for the future to work with.' This 'muscular Christianity' was as important as coal and wealth for the nation's future (2003). Baron de Coubertin founded the modern Olympics to follow that example and redeem French masculinity after the shocks of the Franco-Prussian War. British imperialists clamored for physical education of the working class to heighten fitness for military service during the Boer War (Birley, 1995: 1–2). Hitler and Pétain initiated physical fitness tests to invigorate and ideologize the young in Nazi Germany and Vichy France (Houlihan, 1997: 61–64).

With the onset of the Cold War, a new automotive and office basis to suburban US life, and a suspicion of popular culture and idleness, such policy anxieties and pieties were renewed. A series of influential studies emerged that found flaws in young people's 'muscular strength and flexibility' due to excessive reliance on cars, elevators, and school buses in place of European walking. Accompanied by advertising for trampolines and other sporting equipment, the first and most influential journal article in a whole series called for a national schools exercise program (Kraus and Hirschland, 1953). In 1956, Dwight D. Eisenhower established the President's Council on Youth Fitness in response. Four years later, John F. Kennedy alerted readers of *Sports Illustrated* to a 'growing softness, our increasing lack of physical fitness.' This constituted 'a threat to our security' that must be addressed as per ancient Greece's Olympic training in order to manufacture 'a vigorous state.' After all, 'struggles against aggressors throughout our history have been won on the playgrounds and corner lots and fields of America.' The Soviet alternative/threat could only be defeated by high levels of fitness, a vital counter to 'the television set, the movies and the myriad conveniences and distractions of modern life' (1960). More pessimistically, Richard Nixon's Vice President Spiro Agnew argued that sporting spectatorship and play formed 'one of the few bits of glue that holds society together' (quoted in Lasch, 1979: 202–203).

Functionalist theorists argue that sports provide a physiological, psychological, and sociological outlet for tensions, especially for young men, while team games help form a healthy civil society (Parsons *et al.*, 1955: 129). For Simmel, sports both reflected and incarnated the social order and its disorder (1949), while Durkheim thought they could 'balance and relieve . . . serious life' (1961: 361). And since the first Middletown study in the 1920s announced that high-school loyalties developed and class differences slackened in Muncie, Indiana, with the arrival of basketball, sports have been heralded by Yanqui functionalists for their integrative capacities (Lynd and Lynd, 1956: 212–13, 485).

Male violence is seen as a sociobiological, hormonal danger that can be pacified and redirected through sports. Hence Durkheimians' finding reduced levels of suicide during the Super Bowl and the World Series (Jarvie and Maguire, 1994: 19; Agnew and Petersen, 1989) and Richard Florida, the lead Anglo prelate of creative-industries discourse, drooling over 'soccer moms' showing civic commitment (2009: 268). He argues that the beneficiaries of the postindustrial economy will include cosmopolitan, internationally minded football aficionados (2012: 141).

Those functionalist claims—that sports produce a fitter population, better able to work, more pacific, and capable of expressing powerful feelings in law-abiding ways while standing ready to serve the nation at war—are brought into question by violence on and off the pitch (Salinas Arango, 2018). Richard Hoggart doubted sports' capacity for social control:

> When we say that adolescence must often be a time of opposition and rebellion we should realise that this will often mean *real* rebellion, not something that can be fairly easily piped-off, by providing physical exercise or some kind of strenuous sport or initiative-test.
>
> (1965: 35)

Smiling functionalists neglect the fact that hockey, boxing, hunting, shooting, wrestling, martial arts, football, and motor- and horse-racing all glamorize violence across class and racial fractions. And cross-cultural research indicates more red- and yellow-card sanctions are issued to footballers for violent conduct in countries with high levels of violence than in more pacific locales. This applies to Colombians and Israelis above other nationalities, in both domestic and foreign leagues (Orrego Ramírez *et al.*, 2010; Miguel *et al.*, 2011). No wonder Eisenstein offered a dialectical explanation of football's popularity. It was a 'symbol of joint battle and cooperation' (1987: 284).

Adorno reflected on sports' duality:

> On the one hand, it can have an anti-barbaric and anti-sadistic effect by means of fair play, a spirit of chivalry, and consideration for the weak. On the other hand, in many of its varieties and practices it can promote aggression, brutality, and sadism, above all in people who . . . merely . . . shout from the sideline.
>
> (2010)

For Eco:

> Where man becomes a number in the realm of the organization which has usurped his decision-making role, he has no means of production and is thus deprived of his power to decide. Individual strength, if not exerted in sports activities, is left abased when confronted with the strength of machines which determine man's very movements. In such a society the positive hero must embody to an unthinkable degree the power demands that the average citizen nurtures but cannot satisfy.
>
> (1972: 14)

Orwell famously described sports as 'war minus the shooting,' given their shared ties to violence and imperialism (1945). That pithy description came from his observation of a 'goodwill' British tour by the Soviet football club Дина́мо Москва́ (Dynamo Moscow) (Dmowski, 2015). Orwell feared that such 'sporting contests lead to orgies of hatred' because the competitiveness inherent in football symbolizes and stimulates the desire to defeat the other. His colonial and militia experience of sports in Burma, India, and Spain was of uncontrolled and passionate derision expressed by one section of a crowd towards another.

Rosa Luxemburg metaphorized football to describe weakness in the face of state and military domination (2004: 218). Consider matches between Barcelona and Real Madrid. They have long been supercharged by the Spanish Civil War—the dictatorship's support of Madrid and suppression of Català, and rivalries generated by core-periphery relations. Barça was 'el ejército de un país desarmado' (the military of a disarmed nation) (Vázquez Montalbán, 1987).

Marcuse derided football as a

> conspicuous social mobilization of aggressiveness, the militarization of the affluent society. This mobilization goes far beyond the actual draft

of manpower . . . no longer the "classical" heroizing of killing in the national interest, but rather its reduction to the level of natural events and contingencies of daily life.

(2009: 195)

Bourdieu argued that sports' blend of violence and discipline generated a classic working-class pastime—fatally so in terms of political efficacy (1978). Adorno and Horkheimer made the notorious articulation of 'a left-half at football, a black-shirt, a member of the Hitler Youth, and so on' (1979: 164).

For Iris Marion Young, the idea that a sports club can 'enhance democracy or contribute to a solidarity of strangers' is absurd (2000: 162), while Michael J. Sandel criticizes the aggressive vicariousness on display when touchline parents abuse players, referees, and others (2007: 53). Adorno thought simply watching promoted 'a retrogressive and sometimes even infantile type of person' (1945: 213), as the game's aggression breached the very 'rules of hospitality,' with visiting fans ignored or jeered by their hosts (2005: 118). Guattari said that the fleeting moments of jouissance in football spectatorship, when the self is lost in orgasmic joy through identification with collective triumph, were forever scarred by violent capitalism in their necessary link to an inferior other (1996: 156). Sabine Erika argues that alterity is necessarily produced by the couplet of nationalism and sports, a couplet that works to exclude and denigrate. She emphasizes the connection of nationalism to militarism through a mutual reliance on hierarchy, violence, aggression, and maleness, with sports a key site (1986: 82).

The emergence of *hinchas*/*barras bravas*/*ultras*/hooligans in the 1970s clearly brought functionalism's tidy claims into messy question. For example, Colombia's *barras bravas* include many violent men characterized by:

- bellicose frames of mind
- use of alcohol, marijuana, and cocaine before, during, and after matches
- minimal education
- maximal alienation
- domestic violence; and
- racist stadium chants and taunts

Debates have thrived across Europe and Latin America between those who see redeeming features in this working-class violence, or at least some critical symbolism, and those who condemn it. Progressives argue that unruly crowds may be animated by economic conditions, sexual urges, or blind rage, but also by ideological commitments and desires to comment, maintaining that anomie produces indexically resistive mêlées and criticizing the panoptic design of contemporary stadia (Thompson, 1971; Armstrong, 1998). Conversely, conservatives view hooliganism as the outcome of permissiveness leading to loose-willed, tight-limbed lawlessness (Schimmel *et al.*, 2007; Meneses and González, 2013; Giulianotti, 1999: 80–82).

The reality is probably some mixture of these accounts; British football hooligans appropriated cultural style and social space to compensate for their exclusion from dominant norms, but did so in revolt against difference as much as uniformity, because their solidarity was to do with gender and class sameness expressed against gender and racial difference (Hall, 2016: 195). Either way, the cathectic, febrile fervor and self-righteousness of the sports fan is only equaled or surpassed in the current post-secular conjuncture by true believers in a triumphant faith.

Religion/ideology

Religions are obsessed with when, where, and how they should promote or accept violence, terrifying their followers with visions of a judgmental deity and horrendous punishments dealt out to those who might cross it. Key doctrinal texts and artworks convey these dread fates. Fire, pestilence, pain, injury, suffering, anguish—such words flow almost uncontrollably as one confronts the terror of faith.

Religionists justify their desire to wreak havoc on non-believers or miscreants by promising salvation for those wise and obedient enough to cede power to unearthly creatures that hover above and beyond us, and their self-anointed sacerdotes below. Such magic guarantees deliverance in an afterlife. Conversely, the secular argues for an evaluation based on promises that must be delivered in the real world *during* our existence rather than following it.

Deities are intimately bound to crime and punishment, requiring religionists to 'root . . . out heresy, natural impulses, and evil' (Fanon, 2004: 176). Virtually all faiths justify violence under defined circumstances and a desire for their gods to rule humanity with unquestioned authority (Popovski *et al.*, 2009; Jerryson *et al.*, 2013). Consider ancient Greece's tales of vengeful gods. They match the hypermasculinity of monotheism and the avowedly humanistic world of modernity. Although these fantasies constructed imaginary worlds, they incarnated actual, lived experience: for pantheism, the immense power and threat of the natural world; for monotheism, the historical revolutions led by charismatic figures of authority. For those beholden to the omniscient masculinity of monotheism, there has always been a foundational problem: how to explain the prevalence of violence in all parts of the globe when their faith is in a benevolent and ubiquitous father (Zimbardo, 2007: 38).

True believers rightly claim that secularism is also caught up in violence (Cavanaugh, 2009). This is hardly news: the secular and the religious both seek to exercise authority, power, and control. States and religions take the codification and enactment of violence as fundamental to their very beings, as any glance at doctrines of allegedly just wars or putatively holy tracts will attest (Finlay, 2019; Han, 2018). And prelates of righteous, omniscient deities ready to mete out painful punishment are matched by political theorists and military commanders discerning when and how might is right. Hegel shares with us that 'all that is secular is consequently given over to rudeness and capricious violence' (2001: 127). Conversely, Memmi asserts that 'all religions are intolerant, exclusive, restrictive, and sometimes violent,' even though some adherents may not display such tendencies (2006: 113).

Of course, religions differ, not only among themselves but in terms of space and time. For example, Mazrui notes that contemporary Islam is particularly violent in its political incarnation but can be pacific in its civic role: hence Muslim repression and terrorism on the one hand and numerous safe Islamic cities on the other hand (2014).

In the Global North, the post–Cold War era is dominated by religious anxieties, in part due to the work of Ottoman historian and professional anti-Palestinian Bernard Lewis and Cold War political scientist and Việt Nam War architect Samuel Huntington. In the wake of Sovietism, these two men turned from history and politics to culture. Lewis coined the expression 'clash of civilizations' to capture the difference he discerned between the separation of church and state that had generated US success versus their inter-calculation in Islamic nations, which had supposedly made those countries subordinate (1990). Huntington appropriated the 'clash of civilizations' to argue that future world-historical conflicts would not be 'primarily ideological or primarily economic' but 'cultural' (1993: 22).

This 'cartoon-like world' (Said, 2001) has gained immense media and policy attention since September 11, 2001. Many journalists in the Global North insist on an apocalyptic struggle between good and evil and a bifurcation of the West and Islam. Non-state violence is attributed to Muslims in opposition to freedom and technology, never as the act of subordinated groups against dominant ones. The *New York Times* and *Newsweek* gave Huntington room to account for what had happened. Others adopted it as a legitimate call for empire, from the supposed New Left through to communitarians and the *Economist*. When the US occupation of Iraq entered its third year, commanders and senior non-commissioned officers were required to read Huntington (Rusciano, 2003; Schmitt, 2005).

Study after study has disproven assertions about growing ethnic struggle since the Cold War and a singular Islamic culture opposed to a unitary

Western one. Such claims neglect conflicts over money, property, and politics and cultural differences within the two putative 'blocs' (Fox, 2002; Norris and Inglehart, 2003: 203; United Nations Development Programme, 2004). The clash of civilizations thesis does not work if you apply it to Iran supporting Russia against Chechen rebels and India against Pakistan, for example (Abrahamian, 2003: 535).

What of revolutionary secular ideologies and their complicity with violence? 毛泽东 (Mao Zedong) avowed that

> several hundred million peasants will rise like a mighty storm, like a hurricane, a force so swift and violent that no power, however great, will be able to hold it back. They will smash all the trammels that bind them and rush forward along the road to liberation. They will sweep all the imperialists, warlords, corrupt officials, local tyrants and evil gentry into their graves.
>
> (1971: 24)

The idea of violence as purifying endures because it purportedly produces new ways of living. Hence Engels (1968: 151, 154) and Luxemburg (2004: 64) saying violence is ipso facto political, as private property emerges from it. This history was acknowledged by Malthus, of course, along with many others, who nevertheless regarded it as a necessary evil 'in the early times of all long settled states' (1836: 524). Even the lapsed Parsonian Niklas Luhmann noted that formal property relations put an end to long-lasting conflicts between classes, through violence (2013: 233).

During primitive accumulation, capital embarked on the 'expropriation of the original owners, expulsion of peasants from their land and homes, blockage of access to traditionally available reserves of land, means of subsistence and labour' (Mandel, 1976: 48 n. 7). Sorel (2004) and Michels (1915) viewed the ensuing proletarian violence as a riposte to an ensuing decadence that paradoxically revived the bourgeoisie; but for Marx and Engels, 'the sway of the proletariat' would come with 'violent overthrow of the bourgeoisie' (2006: 19). Владимир Ильич Ленин (Lenin) insisted that 'the liberation of the oppressed class is impossible . . . without a violent Revolution' (2014: 44).

Alongside class, race was always already germane. As Du Bois sorrowfully wrote in 1917:

> We, of the darker peoples, are watching the white world now in mild amaze. Among some of us . . . this sudden descent of Europe into hell has brought unbounded surprise; to others, . . . it has brought the *schaden freude* of the bitterly hurt. But most of us, I judge, look on

silently and sorrowfully, in sober thought, seeing sadly the prophecy of our own souls.

(34)

Sartre saw violence as 'the midwife of history' in his endorsement of 'murderous rampage' as the 'collective unconscious' of the colonized to their subjugation. One must destroy colonial authority in order to 'erase the marks of violence: violence alone can eliminate them' (2004: 117, 127, 135). In Fanon's words, 'decolonization reeks of red-hot cannonballs and bloody knives' (2004: 165), though he recognized that violence was often turned inward by colonized peoples, onto themselves and each other—'internecine violence' (Hawkins, 2003: xviii). This is what Jean Franco aptly and tragically refers to as 'the red thread of violence' (2013: 408), suffusing internal criticism or difference as much as supposed external enemies; part of what she calls 'extreme masculinity' (2013: 56). The liberation psychologist Ignacio Martín-Baró, murdered by Yanqui-backed assassins in El Salvador, put it this way: 'La violencia impuesta por el colonizador es introyectada por el colonizado, quedando anclada en su musculatura como una tensión reprimida y en su mente como una culpabilidad asumida' (The violence imposed by the colonizer is introjected by the colonized, living within his very musculature like a repressed tension, and in his mind as an adopted guilt) (1998: 95).

For Malcolm X, 'the black revolution burns everything that gets in its path' in a process that must be 'destructive and bloody' (2011: 359). Emma Goldman saw political violence as a response to 'accumulated forces in our social and economic life,' akin to nature's 'storm and lightning'; it could 'destroy life and cause great loss' but 'also bring relief' (1917: 1). Allende opposed violence as a means to socialism—other than in response to violence: '¡a la violencia reaccionaria opondremos la violencia revolucionaria!' (We'll oppose reactionary violence with revolutionary violence!) (2018: 26). Lukács derided any notion of class struggle through purely economic transformation as 'vulgar Marxism.' The working class must rebel rather than wait for deliverance through phantasmatic 'natural laws' of economism' (1972: 713–15). On another side of history, Lord Acton, the founding agent of Whig historiography, avowed that 'the supreme conquests of society are won more often by violence than by lenient arts' (1906: 10). Nietzsche regarded violence as crucial to modernity (2002: 78) and Ortega y Gasset as 'reason exasperated' (1930: 50).

But Marcuse famously rejected terrorism as unjustifiable within the terms of a more appropriate 'revolutionary morality,' which sought as its goal 'the liberated individual,' who would refuse 'sneak attacks' (1977: 6). That inevitably leads us to the relationship between demagoguery and violence—a foundational dilemma.

Milton was happy 'to suppress the suppressors themselves,' which was his way of denying Catholics the free-speech rights that he claimed and advocated for his own sect (1869: 78). The United States is often represented as the bastion of free speech, courtesy of its 18th-century Enlightenment project on behalf of white, property-owning men invoked as a model, the locus classicus being the First Amendment.

Mill famously put this argument for contingent free speech:

> Opinions lose their immunity [from sanction], when the circumstances in which they are expressed are such as to constitute their expression a positive instigation to some mischievous act. An opinion that corn-dealers are starvers of the poor, or that private property is robbery, ought to be unmolested when simply circulated through the press, but may justly incur punishment when delivered orally to an excited mob assembled before the house of a corn-dealer.
>
> (1859)

For liberals, the sovereign subject capable of seeking self-determination up to the point of adversely affecting others is a gold standard. They are happy, for example, to restrict freedom of speech in order to constrain violence, because of the harm done to others. Hate speech poses difficulties for them, since it is deemed irrelevant to the victim's ability to select 'roles and identities,' unlike speech inflaming assault or war (Sandel, 1998: xiv–xv). So whereas YouTube and the South African state both link hate speech to violence, the European Court of Human Rights does not.[1]

This is the equivalent of 'sticks and stones may break my bones but words will never hurt me.' It fails to draw links between hate speech aimed at one's status as member of a group and how that is tied to historic, current, future, and internalized discrimination and violence. Conversely, the Organization of Islamic Cooperation,[2] which represents 57 Muslim countries, subordinates other international protocols to شريعة (Shari'ah) and describes 'Islamophobia' as 'the worst form of terrorism.' Members generally walk out of global gatherings that address queer rights (Howden *et al.*, 2006; Wahab, 2007; Evans, 2012).

That organization is very exercised by blasphemy: attacks on religious icons or defamation of their dutiful adherents. Yet the القرآن (Qu'ran) does not prescribe punishments for blasphemy or prohibit representation of its true believers' favorite prophet. Islamic states that prohibit blasphemy are generally authoritarian and experience violent resistance by their subjects. Nilay Saiya looked at terrorism within Muslim nations between 1991 and 2013. Countries that enforced blasphemy laws had more Islamist terrorist attacks than those without such legislation (2017).

Bhikhu Parekh's sensible blend of history and theory alerts us that

> violence is one of the most important factors in accentuating identity consciousness. It threatens one's very survival because of how one is defined by others, and leaves one no choice but to unite with and against others on that basis. This is why the racial, religious and other forms of violence polarize communities and individuals very quickly, and lead both to an obsessive preoccupation with and an exclusive definition of the relevant identity.
>
> (2008: 26)

Hegemonic ideas about identity have always mattered—and been connected to collective violence. They informed imperial expansion through the religious, civilizational fervor of Spain's *conquista de América*, Portugal's *missão civilizadora*, and France and Britain's *mission civilisatrice* as Western Europe sought to remake the globe in its own phantasmatic image (Rojas, 2002).

With physical conquest came linguistic and hence codified rule. Queen Isabella's functionaries established Castilian as a mode of conquest and management. Indeed, her imperial grammarian argued that 'language was always the companion of empire.' Along with Christianity, it would enable the queen to 'put under her yoke many barbarous peoples and nations of alien languages' (de Nebrija, 2016: 202, 204). In 1513, an early Spanish excursion carried a manifesto for indigenous people from a theological committee. It narrated world history through the anointing of Peter as Christ's vicar on Earth, which was used to justify later popes dividing up the world. The document concluded with a chilling warning of what would happen in the event of resistance to imperial conquest: women and children would be enslaved, their goods seized, and culpability laid at the feet of the vanquished. So overt are its precepts, its careful attention to ideology, its alibi in divine nomination, and its overtly political use of non-combatants as symbols, that this is a remarkably modern text. Of course, Christianity is non-modern, and the text's mode of address incantatory. But it is also reasoned in its brutality: fire and the sword will prevail, so follow instructions and you will be spared. The Spanish did not present themselves as superior, but simply as selected by God's delegate (Brown, 2000: 203–205)—and once the Crown appreciated the 'demographic collapse' of war and disease imported to Latin America, it encouraged higher indigenous birth rates to convert a flock and create a workforce (Colmenares, 1996; Braudel, 1984: 393).

The conquerors' use of superior military technology and ideology to transfer beliefs and seize goods was a model for much European practice, something wryly troped in the postcolonial African saying that 'when the white man came he had the Bible and we had the land. When the white man left we had the Bible and he had the land' (quoted in McMichael, 1996: 17). If colonial efforts directed at rural development failed, this was deemed to be because 'peoples of low social efficiency' predominated. They required either extermination or ideological transformation (aka Christianity) (Kidd, 2009: 311)—hence Hegel avowing that Native Americans 'gradually vanished at the breath of European activity' (2001: 98). That 'breath' may indeed have introduced new diseases, but it also aspirated through ammunition and killing—and an insistence on the radical separateness of cultures and the superiority of one of them. To examine those doctrines of supremacy, we need to account for gender and nation.

Notes

1 www.echr.coe.int/Documents/FS_Hate_speech_ENG.pdf.
2 www.oic-oci.org/oicv3/page/?p_id=52&p_ref=26&lan=en.

3 Gender

Violence is foundational to gender, and vice versa. Following some introductory remarks about relevant theories, this chapter's case studies examine a crisis in US masculinity (the Bobbitt cut), men and sports (notably Pat Tillman's legend), Latin American culture, and an *ur*-figure of imagined violent masculinity (007).

If a monopoly on legitimate violence characterizes the state in Weberian terms, then patriarchy is created and sustained because 'males continue to monopolize the techniques and technology of physical violence' (Harris, 1991: 182). For most of history, only men have been welcome as citizens, though women were crucial servants of polities. Aristotle reasoned that as 'the state is made up of households, before speaking of the state, we must consider the management of the household,' which he defined as the homologous relationships of masters to slaves, husbands to wives, and parents to children (1963: 62–63). Citizens relied on women and slaves to undertake physical and emotional labor in the classical era of the ancient world, sequestering politics to themselves (Lister, 1997).

The founders of the US Constitution regarded women, slaves, children, the insane, and the un-propertied as incapable of independent, disinterested thought. The state was to be funded through taxes on property. As a consequence, only the landed were really committed to the society that it would govern. Over the next 50 years, proletarian militancy successfully pushed for an end to a franchise based on property. White men obtained the vote. Women and people of color continued to be subordinated politically in a way that was overtly analogous to their domestic and industrial situations (McHugh, 1999: 38–39; Duggan, 2003: 5) and relied on for their emotional as well as physical labor. So, alarmed by 'mob violence,' Lincoln insisted that a 'political religion' of 'reverence of the law' must be 'breathed by every American mother, to the lisping babe, that prattles on her lap' (1838).

It took lengthy, titanic struggles to endow those households' adult occupants caring for lisping babes with equivalent political subjectivities to men's, so fundamental were the control of women, children, sex, and every-day life to the allocation of political-economic resources (Benhabib, 2002: 83). These subordinate souls were subject in most societies to 'the domestic authority of the head of the household,' as the 16th-century philosopher Jean Bodin approvingly put it (1994: 87). This subordination was partly a reaction against what Aristotle and Machiavelli alike saw as the threat to governance posed by women's procreative and symbolic power, which could drive rulers to injudicious acts when their sexual honor/ownership was threatened; hence Machiavelli's meditation 'How States are Ruined by Women' (1950: 488–89).

For many political philosophers, gender has represented a struggle between 'authority and attachment,' with women blamed for a supposed over-emphasis on the family that diminishes the energies required for civic participation (Shapiro, 2001: 2–4). Kant derided the easy life of indolent 'immaturity' over Enlightenment responsibilities, while suggesting 'the entire fair sex' would find the 'step forward to maturity' beyond them (1991: 54). Pufendorf seemed to celebrate that 'states have certainly been formed by men, not women' (2000: 125).

Endless recitations of what counts as virtuous citizenship emphasize military life, a traditionally male preserve of violence in the service of the nation that superintends and delimits democracy and authority, constituting a privileged area of welfare provision by contrast with state expenditures on women and the young (Watson, 2004: 7). Classical and modern political theory alike assume and even endorse domestic violence, warlike masculin-ity, and the notion that 'real' politics is generated, discussed, and finalized between guys (Brown, 1988).

Unsurprisingly, many accounts of the social order take masculinity as their touchstone. Consider the Oedipal myth: a man whose feet have been brutally bound and disfigured as a child by his father unwittingly carries out a prediction by killing his father and marrying his mother. On discovering the fact, Oedipus tears his eyes out. This story is used to explain the transfer of adolescent boys' affection from mothers to other women and processes of succession and rivalry in male life. It takes violence as the narrative touch-stone of masculinity (Badinter, 1995).

René Girard proposes a tripartite and mimetic character to male desire, 'not only a subject and an object but a third presence as well: the rival.' Both subject and rival want that object. This is not due to its innate proper-ties. Rather, the rival's desire 'alerts the subject to the desirability of the object.' Girard identifies sacrificial violence as the key to holding together social formations that lack a fully achieved juridical apparatus. A subject is selected, onto whom the tensions of a group can be projected: sometimes an enemy and sometimes a friend. This sacrificial figure is a surrogate (1992).

These are only some of the manifold discourses that either regard male violence as a given, a tragic burden of pain, or a cultural norm. Carol Gilligan notes that where the 'feminist movement has held men responsible for their violence and privilege,' the 'mythopoetic men's movement has embraced men as wounded' (1997).

For Jacqueline Rose, women's sexuality troubles and defies masculinity. As she puts it, 'honour killing is the cruelest modern exemplar of how the sexuality of women can provoke a patriarchal anguish which knows no limits in the violent lengths it will go to assuage itself' (2014: 11). This world lets 'women be fearful so men can feel brave and safe' (2014: 32). Irigaray says that for men, 'the encounter with the other outside the self, especially the different other . . . will no longer be taken into consideration and joined except in breaking down prohibitions, with a certain amount of violence' (2004: 93).

Raewyn Connell articulates the history of imperialism with contemporary gender politics. She finds Western European and North American white male sexuality isomorphic with power: men seek global dominion and desire, orchestrated to oppress women via hegemonic masculinity. This encompasses obvious sexism—rape, domestic violence, and obstacles to female occupational advancement—and more subtle domination, such as excluding women from social environments and sports teams, and the bourgeois media's fascination with men (1987, 1998, 2001, 2005). Men who feel socially weak (the working class, minorities, and immigrants) may find the hegemonic model appealing. But the real sources of their powerlessness lie in the monetary and racial economy, not struggles against women and the queer (Messner, 1997: 7–8, 12; Rowe, 1997: 124).

Of course, straight, strong, domineering masculinity oppresses the many men excluded from it, while even 'subscribers' often find its norms unattainable; and there are many opponents. The articulation of hegemonic masculinity against women and queers makes it unpopular with vast numbers of people. Connell acknowledges that male identity is complex and polyvalent, with no singular set of qualities consistently marked as masculine. Masculinity and men's bodies (symbolically conceived as unitary) are contested sites, fraught with contradictions (1998).

As long ago as the 17th century, Pufendorf blamed the rapist rather than the victim/survivor, even if he required the latter to show prudence to the point of fear as part of her daily conduct:

> If a virgin should be compelled through force to lend her limbs to the lustful action of a stronger person whose violence she is unable to ward off from herself, nothing can be imputed to her for that reason.
>
> (1994: 71)

But the idea of masculine virtue being tied to violence, be it in defense of faith, family, or frontier, is immensely strong. Machiavelli insisted that men dressed in uniform and trained to fight must lose any 'customs [they] deem to be effeminate' (1520: 1). From protective dueling knights to endless military campaigns allegedly waged in the name of women, the 'right' way of doing violence births ideas of nobility. Ironically, women's rights are often invoked to justify projects that are quite unrelated to them. For example, the British utilized traditional limitations on women's freedom and education to legitimize the colonization of India (Mackie, 2012).

Wherever you look, from diplomats to bombardiers to correspondents, war is an implicitly and explicitly male activity. This is rarely recognized in mainstream media coverage and academic knowledge, or problematized as such (Sjoberg, 2013; Ackerly *et al.*, 2006; Hearn, 2012; von der Lippe and Ottosen, 2016). That said, reactionary commentators, male and female alike, valorized the hypermasculinity that was unleashed beyond even its normal limits in the United States after 2001, specifically highlighting ideas of male chivalry, domination, and certainty. Camille Paglia, Peggy Noonan, and Coulter mandated a fulsome heterosexuality (Cole, 2008: 123–24; Miller, 2013). These public intellectuals, who command column inches and video clips, took the opportunity presented by war to push a domestic agenda in favor of male power, using international relations to denounce queerness and feminism. On this account, masculine valor expresses itself through bloodshed and leadership. It is incarnated in the military as a righteous national embodiment of power, spirit, religiosity, and victory.

Of course, the claim that women are naturally nurturing or pacific by contrast with men has not stood up to a multitude of counterexamples, from feminist guerrillas to women who are violent to children (Rayas Velasco, 2009; Enloe, 1983; Feinman, 2000). For example, polling indicates that many Colombians endorse personal and systematic violence alike. Half the urban population believes in taking force into their own hands and killing to protect their families. A third favors corporal punishment against children (Guerrero and Fandiño-Losada, 2017). It is estimated that 39% of Colombian children under the age of 4 have suffered such physical assault at home (Cuartas, 2018). And while Law 294 of 1996 only permits parents to 'correct them and sanction them moderately,' Civil Code 1883 allows 'violent punishment in the home' (Global Initiative, 2018).

But female violence is in no way symmetrical with male militarism. Feminist theories of international relations stress the significance of gender at structural and interpersonal levels, from across the world system to internal dynamics within nations, including the masculine priorities and personalities that drive conflicts (Riley *et al.*, 2008; Peterson, 1992). Clearly, while women have been granted intense value as symbols of the nation (think of representations of woman-as-nation or the systematic rape of women by men by invading armies or ethnic majorities), only decades of struggle translated this into anything like full political inclusiveness, and generally not in taking decisions about waging war.

US masculinity

Let's consider a limit case of gendered domestic violence: the 1993 story of John Wayne Bobbitt and Lorena Bobbitt. Following what appears to have been coercive sex, Lorena cut off her husband's penis as he slept, then drove to the home of her boss. Lorena later told *20/20* (1978–present) that she had difficulty negotiating tight right-hand turns en route: 'I try to turn, but then I saw that I have it in my hand.' She threw the penis out of the car. The police heard about the episode from both parties and took off in search of the organ. Once found, it was packed in a plastic bag, taken to a hospital, and reattached. James Sehn, a surgeon involved in the operation, reported countless demands from women to see before-and-after photographs. And 'July 13, 1993, will be remembered as the day the word penis appeared in 30-point type in *The New York Times*' (Safire, 1994). Network news referred to it only as 'the appendage' (Moore, 2019).

This extremely isolated emasculatory incident produced a search by journalists for a new, dangerous feminism supposedly connected to Valerie Solanas's 'Society for Cutting Up Men' manifesto (1983)—a ridiculous quest given the limited concern expressed by some women for the alleged rape of Ms. Bobbitt, mixed with horror at her retributive method.

Subsequent law cases saw the parties acquitted: John of marital rape, Lorena of malicious wounding. CNN broadcast her case, during which Ms. Bobbitt's lawyers argued her life was worth more than his penis. Mr. Bobbitt sold T-shirts emblazoned with 'A Cut Heard around the World,' 'Love Hurts,' and 'Severed Part.' He informed viewers of *Jenny Jones* (1991–2003) that Lorena had 'tried to destroy me in the worst way possible.' (The program showed a video of their wedding, holding on a frame of her cutting the cake.) Howard Stern held a New Year's Eve telethon on his behalf. Lorena's supporters mimicked the motion of scissors with their hands for news cameras. Paglia renamed the act 'the Boston Tea Part.' The Jurassic Penis company offered a 'Penis Protection Plan,' complete with full cloning service. *Martha Stuart's Better Than You at Entertaining*—a parody of Martha Stewart books—included circumcision menus. A porn film starring Mr. Bobbitt reenacted his domestic and hospital experiences from that historic summer's night. He ended the year with a heavily publicized operation to extend the length of his penis by three inches and its width by one inch (Miller, 1998). Twenty-five years later, Amazon Prime spliced together archival footage as part of its four-part series, *Lorena* (2019), one of many tropes:

> In Philip Roth's misanthropic master piece *Sabbath's Theater* (1995), in David Fincher's *Fight Club* (1999), also a misanthropic masterpiece, and in the Eminem song 'Evil Twin' (2013), among other unlikely places, including a field guide to marine invertebrates. (It has a namesake worm, one that attacks prey with jaws that resemble scissors.)
>
> (Anolik, 2018)

The incident is shocking for its mutual sexual violence and the sense of taboos being broken—the removal of genitals, their almost casual discarding, the nervously jokey way in which the story was told and troped, and people from the popular classes put under the mocking microscope of mainstream media. It captured the incipient male violence that is always a threat, but very occasionally subject to one almighty, rarely invoked, retributive sanction. Such limit cases alert us to how striking it is when male power is so frankly confronted by seemingly cowed women.

Sports

As we saw in the previous chapter, sports have been crucial sites for training and expressing male violence, both on and off the field. Functionalists throw their milk and cookies in the air when confronting the record of assault by athletes. It includes dozens of professional US football players charged with domestic violence as well as high-profile murder cases. Michael Messner argues that

> football, based as it is on the most extreme possibilities of the male body . . . is clearly a world apart from women, who are relegated to the role of cheerleaders/sex objects on the sidelines. . . . In contrast to the bare and vulnerable bodies of the cheerleaders, the armored bodies of the football players are elevated to mythical status.
>
> (1990: 213)

Such stars are constituted as models for emulation, displacing the traditional role of sovereign royalty as symbols of higher conduct. They form a labor aristocracy: people from working-class backgrounds who become fleetingly wealthy and famous at a young age and flicker as incendiary but ephemeral signs of class mobility. At the same time, they are paid to play a sport that emphasizes coaching control and minimizes player autonomy (Evens and Lefever, 2011; Lipsyte, 2011).

There are also disturbing correlations between international soccer's fandom and domestic violence: during the 2014 and 2018 men's World Cup finals, the rate of such assaults in Colombia rose by 38% and 25% respectively during matches involving the national team. The figure was 50% for the 2015 Copa América, a competition between national teams from the region (Salazar, 2018).

Discussion of athletes' sexual violence is often accompanied by a bizarre critique of women. Jeffrey Benedict says these men have had 'their power of self-restraint eroded by excessive sexual indulgence,' which has produced 'increasingly deviant sexual habits.' Women who willingly have sex with men outside marriage are accused by Benedict of 'complicity' in the 'jock-groupie tango . . . the engine driving . . . an image of women as sexually compliant.' Surprise, surprise: men are beasts who need to fuck all the time, and 'bad girls' who initiate sex with various partners are responsible for the mistreatment of 'good girls,' because they encourage men to pursue 'a deviant lifestyle.' The same notion of 'bad girls' is evident in *Sports Illustrated*'s account of professional athletes who father children across liaisons (also discussed in a *New York Times* editorial). 'Wherever there's money there are going to be women' is a refrain. A chaplain to the San Francisco Giants (baseball) and the 49ers (football) referred to 'women who hunt,' while the National Football League's (NFL) early 21st-century 'rookie orientation' featured 'former NFL groupies' explaining 'how they seduced players' (Begel and Baum, 2000: 50–51; Benedict, 1998: xi–xii, 1–2; Wahl and Wertheim, 1998: 67–68, 71; 'Irresponsible,' 1998).

A revised NFL 'Rookie Transition' offers 'Social responsibility for players,' warning them about both domestic violence and sexual assault.[1] In 2014, a Players Association Commission on Violence Prevention was formed, but Deborah Epstein, its domestic-violence expert, soon resigned, deriding the Commission as 'a fig leaf' (quoted in Simon and Bowman, 2018). The league may claim to teach about 'social responsibility,' but its official history speaks of evolving the typical athlete 'from "everyman" to "superman."'[2]

That obverse to cautionary tales—the militaristic heroization of US sportsmen—specializes in nationalistic hypermasculinity, which has been coordinated with the military since the American War in Việt Nam. Consider the Armed Forces Bowl,[3] a college football competition sponsored by Lockheed Martin. Lockheed is one of the vast array of companies whose livelihoods rely on corporate welfare via the private development and public-sector purchase of murderous technology. In this instance, promotional activities are not about selling products to fans, as per most sports underwriting. They are dedicated to creating goodwill towards militaristic welfare through broad-brush suburbanite homologies constructed between sport, nation, and matériel, and feature ghoulish recruiters preying on young spectators and the 'Great American Patriot Award' (Butterworth and Moskal, 2009).[4] Enter Patrick Daniel Tillman.

Having been an Arizona State University (ASU) athlete, Pat Tillman had a successful NFL stint with the Arizona Cardinals, but then he turned down a USD 3.6 million contract in favor of joining the military; he had interpreted September 11, 2001 as justification for retribution. That decision became a crucial aspect of US propaganda. Tillman was sent a public note of congratulation by Secretary of Defense Donald Rumsfeld ('Mary Tillman,' 2008). His recruitment delivered a 'testosterone cocktail' to the state that 'was impossible to resist' (Zirin, 2005). Reporters 'simply could not write about Tillman without evoking his role as a protagonist of mythic proportions' (Chidester, 2009: 366).

When he died in Afghanistan in April 2004, Tillman was immediately hailed for his sacrifice by the state, academia, the NFL, and the bourgeois media. He was posthumously awarded a Silver Star for 'gallantry in action against an armed enemy' he had supposedly pursued and 'forced to withdraw' (Couric, 2008). Senator John McCain gave a eulogy at Tillman's nationally televised funeral, quickly turning the occasion into a hymn to 'our blessed and mostly peaceful society,' supported of course by military service, where 'the purpose of all good courage is love.' McCain said that soldiers' 'blood debts' and 'goodness' would endure, and reassured Tillman's family it would 'see him again, when a loving god reunites us all' (2004). This courage and these debts had driven Tillman from football to fighting, according to this ideologue—who had never met him, and whose 'thoughts' were immediately published by the far-right *National Review* magazine. Coulter called Tillman 'an American original—virtuous, pure and masculine like only an American male can be' who 'died bringing freedom and democracy to 28 million Afghans' (2004). The Cato Institute took his volunteerism as a sign that a military draft was not necessary, so pure was the population's desire to serve the nation while sidestepping the state (Healy, 2004).

The White House hailed Tillman as 'an inspiration on and off the football field . . . who made the ultimate sacrifice in the war on terror' (quoted in Zirin, 2005). The governor of Arizona ordered that flags at ASU be flown at half-mast, and the university marketed match tickets under his name. The Cardinals divined that he 'represented all that was good in sports,' placing his uniform in a glass case alongside bouquets and teddy bears. The league said Tillman 'personified all the best values of his country and the NFL.' Much was said of his non-stop energy and desire to hurt opponents in tackles (quoted in 'Tillman Killed,' 2004).

But as time passed, Tillman's story became more complex and contradictory. He was an atheist, as his youngest brother Richard explained to

McCain and ESPN at the funeral: 'Pat isn't with God. He's fucking dead. He wasn't religious. So thank you for your thoughts, but he's fucking dead' (quoted in Tillman and Zacchino, 2008). And during his time abroad, Tillman had become anti-war and a fan of Noam Chomsky—had he returned from theater, he was going to meet the veteran analyst of imperialism (Zirin, 2005). Then it turned out that Tillman had been the victim of manslaughter by his colleagues, not murder by his enemies. In short, he failed the tasks laid down for him by history—he was not what he looked like or what the war machine had manufactured, but a critic of US imperialism at the very moment that he was celebrated as its epigone and epitome. Pat Tillman had gone from sporting recruit to nationalistic recruit to ideological recruit to dead refusenik.

General Stanley McChrystal is notorious for several things, foremost among them having been Barack Obama's chief warmonger of Afghanistan and a key long-term operative in US military mistreatment of detainees. He was also a central player in the scandalous, mendacious propagandistic use of Tillman's name, service, and death. When McChrystal was appointed to run the empire in Afghanistan, Tillman's father accused him of having conducted 'a falsified homicide investigation.' Tillman's brother Kevin called him a 'fraud,' because McChrystal had approved the award of a Silver Star to Pat, despite the Ranger's death having occurred at the hands of compatriots (which McChrystal admitted under oath that he had known, even though the citation referred to 'devastating enemy fire'). In 2007, the Pentagon's acting inspector general held McChrystal 'accountable for the inaccurate and misleading assertions' in that citation, but was overruled by the army ('Parents of Slain,' 2009; 'Mary Tillman,' 2008; Laidlaw and Mendoza, 2007; Krakauer, 2009; Tillman with Zacchino, 2008; Tillman, 2017). The military later determined that the Silver Star was 'based on what he [Tillman] intended to do' (White, 2005).

Tillman's family spent years trying to penetrate the Pentagon's obfuscation and propaganda in order to establish what had been known from the moment of his death—that he'd been killed by Yanquis, heroized by Yanquis, and used by Yanquis through their state in a way that was first and foremost dedicated to lying to his family members (Collier, 2005; Camacho and Hauser, 2007; Andrews, 2006). As second-order meaning, it bought into a long and disgraceful association of whiteness with sporting and military valor (Kusz, 2007).

Tillman's brother and fellow recruit Kevin testified before Congress that impending disclosures about atrocities committed by US forces at Abu Ghraib (Hersh, 2004) had driven the Pentagon to clutch at Pat and claim him for nationalism:

Revealing that Pat's death was a fratricide would have been a political disaster during a month already swollen with political disasters and a brutal truth that the American public would undoubtedly find unacceptable, so the facts needed to be suppressed. An alternative narrative had to be constructed.

(quoted in 'Mary Tillman,' 2008)

Kevin went on to explain how repulsed the family was to learn that 'our elected leaders were subverting international law and humanity' through the seizure and torture of people. He noted that 'suspension of Habeas Corpus is supposed to keep this country safe' but that 'reason is being discarded for faith, dogma, and nonsense' (Tillman, 2006).

Any attempt to rearticulate Pat Tillman's death and its faux heroization led to calumny from the right. When ASU art professor John Jota Leaños generated a poster of Tillman titled 'Friendly Fire,' questioning these militaristic distortions 'and the quasi-religious and dogmatic adherence to Tillman's mythological heroic image by mainly conservative male Americans,' he was subjected to scrutiny by CBS, CNN, and ABC. That produced angry outbursts by viewers, hundreds of violent, splenetic emails and threats, an inquiry into Leaños by ASU, and his denunciation by school bureaucrats (Leaños, 2005).[5]

When the *San Francisco Chronicle* disclosed that Tillman had regarded the invasion of Iraq as 'fucking illegal' (Collier, 2005), Coulter thundered 'I don't believe it' (quoted in Zirin, 2005). There was even an embarrassingly performative, sentimental academic lament for him that fretted over the loss of US servicemen, as if *they* were the central sufferers of imperial overreach (Lockford, 2008).

Kevin Tillman noted to Congress that querying the official rendition of his brother's death was equated with 'casting doubt on Pat's bravery and sacrifice.' It was nothing of the sort. Rather, once the nature of the scandal was exposed, 'Pat was no longer of use as a sales asset.' Rumsfeld did not contact the family once this 'asset' had been compromised, but he did deny there had been a cover-up. His typically torturous prose found the story had been 'handled in a way that was unsatisfactory.' This was an oblique reference to the fact that Tillman's mother learned her son was the victim of fratricide from the *Arizona Republic*, not an Arizona Republican. For questioning the Pentagon, she and her surviving sons were derided by the right. One of the army's principal investigators and a recommender of the Silver Star award, Tillman's commander Ralph Kauzlarich, suggested that the bereaved family had been unable to accept that this was 'an unfortunate accident' because it was not religious and hence saw Pat's fate as to become 'worm dirt.' (This 'reasoning' was also evident in an internal military memo

[Breslau, 2008].) At least Tillman's worm-afterlife had a name: the Afghan soldier killed alongside him was left unidentified for years (Fish, 2006; Goff, 2006; 'Mary Tillman,' 2008; Couric, 2008; Breslau, 2008; Greenwald, 2007). Such are the wages of a masculinity glorified then discarded, as Amir Bar-Lev's *The Tillman Story* (2010) showed in its meticulous documentation of the family's struggle for truth. Meanwhile, Kauzlarich's reward was a successful hagiography, *The Good Soldiers* (Finkel, 2009).

When Wittgenstein problematized the seemingly synonymous use of the word 'good' in the formulations, 'a good football player' and 'a good fellow,' he was referring to the complexities that arise when words are redisposed to connote ethical value rather than empirical description (1965). That category mistake bedeviled the US government when it misappropriated Pat Tillman's life and death, overwhelmed by the actuality of his sporting career and the fantasy of his military one.

Latin America

Cross-cultural research has established strong correlations between domestic violence and anti-feminist, sexist attitudes (Herrero *et al.*, 2017). Violence against women is more common in Latin America than most parts of the world, as are female deaths from firearms (Small Arms Survey, 2016). The region's many extreme forms of violence feature rape, disfigurement, and femicide (Moloney, 2015; Huertas and Jiménez, 2016). At the same time as gendered violence typically takes place within established relationships, sexual assaults on mass transit soar in many regions. Where I live, in Mexico City, the problem has been so bad for so long that women and children have their own carriages on the metro and delineated areas of the Metrobus system.

This relates to popular discourse as well as street and domestic violence. Consider the term *chingar*. It is used to describe every kind of abuse, pleasure, or failure. Somewhat akin to 'fuck' or 'shit' in English, *chingar* is polysemic. But its origins lie in penetrating, humiliating, possessing, and raping: 'violence rules darkly over all the meanings of the word.' *La chingada* in particular is demeaned and dismissed as 'an inert heap of bones, blood and dust' (Paz, 1961: 76–77, 85).

This in turn relates to *machismo* (with which readers may be familiar) and *Marianismo*, which is less discussed outside the region. Generations of Latin Americans have been raised with *machismo* and *Marianismo* as ways of life. These dual mythologies of masculinity and femininity restrict women's economic opportunities and daily conduct ('Wonder Women,' 2015). Both ideologies are associated with Latin America, though some critics have traced their origins to peninsular Europe (Stevens, 1973). They clearly derive from the sexual violence and forced marriages that were part of imperial and colonial experience (Strasser and Tinsman, 2010) and the Roman Catholic family ideal of an unseen, judgmental father (God) and an ever-present, caring mother (Mary).

Men are represented as eternal sons who need to be interpreted and cared for by their mothers. Because each man remains forever basically a child, his actions are beyond his own willpower to control. He cannot be held accountable or punished for aberrant conduct; instead, he must be understood and forgiven (Wills, 2011). Within this governing rhetoric, differences of course abound, notably a hypersexualized narrative of the unruly, rapacious, dark-skinned man versus the business-like, controlled, lighter-skinned one (Viveros, 2013). Both concepts permeate all levels of society, granting men a form of entitlement to symbolic and physical violence. This is a classic instantiation of hegemonic masculinity, but reaches further than the norms of the Global North (Pineda Duque, 2003; Connell, 2003).

Marianismo sets up the Virgin Mary as the ideal for women, who are expected to uphold two key principles that she putatively embodied: chastity prior to motherhood and motherhood itself. These precepts are designed not only as everyday guides but as the sole purposes of a woman's life, for which she is willing to sacrifice everything and anything, including her sense of self. South America's mythic 19th-century liberator, Simón Bolívar, famously declared that Latin American men were blinded by liberty and pulchritude alike, with women offering a surfeit of pleasure and nature, a fetishized sexuality that must be resisted by men: 'freedom is as dangerous as beauty in women, whom all seek to seduce out of love, or vanity' (2003: 102)

Consider Colombia. The nation's Instituto Colombiano de Medicina Legal (Colombian Institute of Legal Medicine) reported 21,115 cases of sexual violence in 2014, with 85.05% of victims being women (2015). As in many countries, over 90% of homicide victims are men, but unlike women, generally not as a consequence of violence undertaken at home, or with a sexual element. Women are frequently killed by people they know—attacked by family members rather than strangers (De la Hoz Bohórquez and Romero Quevedo, 2016). A full 39% of Colombian women report violent treatment from male partners, and a spate of acid attacks by men on women over the last five years has affected thousands ('Wonder Women,' 2015; 'Alarma y repudio,' 2014; Guerrero, 2013; Gaviria Castellanos *et al.*, 2015). Public health experts argue that a failure to consider historical patterns of oppression results in discounted statistics of such violence (Bello-Urrego, 2013).

All sides in Colombia's quasi-military conflict have engaged in sexual torture, with women and sexual minorities targeted for humiliation as part of a violent clearance aimed at sex workers, street retailers, and other people on the margins of power who are assaulted by armed groups in public space (Suárez Pinzón, 2015; Oxfam, 2009; Serrano-Amaya, 2018). Colombia Diversa estimates that over 1,000 queer people were killed between 1993 and 2017. A high proportion of victims remain unidentified, and perpetrators free.[6] Statutory rape is routine practice for guerrilla and *paramilitares* alike (Human Rights Watch, 2019).

The International Organization for Migration details in all seriousness Colombia's national legislation forbidding sexual violence (Organización Internacional para las Migraciones, 2015); influential thinkers with no ethnographic, political-economic, or statistical experience of the country like John Rawls praise it for non-coercive policies protecting women (1999: 110); and the government provides impressive-looking reports to the UN's Committee on the Elimination of All Forms of Discrimination against Women (2017). But everyone knows this is one more case where policing, the courts, and everyday life are distant from such ideals and claims—in semiotic terms, *langue* versus *parole*.

Sex work and child exploitation

There is considerable feminist controversy over adult sex work, both locally and transnationally, and its relationship to violence. For many, it represents and perpetuates the subordination of women to men, women's bodies as currency, and riskiness as a way of (an imposed) life. This abolitionist position originated in a mixture of 19th-century feminism, evangelical Christianity, and racialized concerns that young white US women were being seized and trafficked to the Global South. There is little evidence to support the contention that such slavery was widespread. The movement is commonly understood to have been a moral panic about gendered modernity: women on the move, nationally and internationally, largely of their own accord (O'Brien *et al.*, 2013; Soderlund, 2011).

The sex industry today involves millions of workers (mostly female) and customers (mostly male). Abolitionists regard this proliferation as evidence of a quasi-enslavement that should be eradicated. The bourgeois Anglo media tend to constitute 'good' versus 'bad' classes of sex worker—the trafficked versus the voluntarist, as per Alexandra Kollontai's lament that sex work 'is an act of violence by the woman upon herself in the name of material gain' (1978: 275). Conversely, advocates regard sexual labor as a material reality of agency as well as a form of exploitation that must be managed, in the same way as the sale of human labor power via the body is governed in other sectors of the economy, such as cleaning or nursing. For these advocates, the voices of women sex workers should be heard, their perils minimized, and global variations in state protection and collective experience taken into account (Della Giusta *et al.*, 2008; O'Brien *et al.*, 2013; Bennett, 2016; Agustín, 2007; Nussbaum, 1999).

This becomes a very different controversy when allied to child labor and sexual exploitation, where there is universal denunciation of statutory rape. Such exploitation of children is global and profitable. Unlike most trafficking, it generally involves mobility by offenders rather than victims (Bang *et al.*, 2014).

The UN's World Tourism Network on Child Protection[7] has been running under various names since 1997. Research from the Fundación Renacer,[8] the Instituto Colombiano de Bienestar Familiar (Colombian Institute of Family Welfare),[9] and numerous academics demonstrates the level of child sexual exploitation (Díaz Granados and Rodríguez Cruz, 2006; Bernal-Camargo *et al.*, 2013; Mosquera and Bozzi, 2005; Londoño *et al.*, 2014).[10] They argue that between 30,000 and 40,000 Colombian children and adolescents have been victims of 'Explotación sexual commercial de niños, niñas, y adolescentes (ESCNNA)' (commercial sexual exploitation of boys, girls, and adolescents) (Guerrero-Figueroa Guerrero, 2016).

Current estimates are that Cartagena de Indias has well over 1,000 children and adolescents trafficked to tourists—70% of them girls—and thousands of children involved in pornography. These statistics are widely regarded as understating reality, due to the stigma involved and the fact that perhaps 90% of perpetrators act with impunity. Most are gangsters, illicit miners, or tourists (Moloney, 2018). The Fundación Renacer correlates increased child sexual exploitation in Cartagena with resource booms (2016). There is some evidence that children from poor, violent homes find sex work to be an improvement on their daily lives and sense of agency (Camacho Ordoñez and Trujillo González, 2009). And although the core of the industry is foreign adult men seeking sex with female Colombian children, the demand extends to queer male minors, some of whom enter prostitution following familial rejection of their sexuality (Castillo Murillejo and Rivera Reyes, 2013). As in other countries with similar trends, there is a high incidence of coercion and sexually transmitted disease among the exploited; the Caribbean has the world's highest rate of HIV/AIDS after sub-Saharan Africa (Baral *et al.*, 2012; Djellouli and Quevedo-Gómez, 2015). One sex worker put it this way: 'the Spanish built these walls to protect this city. But nobody protected me' (quoted in Charles, 2018).

The sexual exploitation of children begins in liminal contact zones: taxi rides, concierge desks, and plazas, inter alia, are switching points between tourist arrivals and child rape, providing information about the trade and articulation into it (Arango Arias and Hurtado Díaz, 2012). The *Economist* notes that 'almost any taxi driver will offer to hook male passengers up with prostitutes, and some of the city's major hotels are lax in allowing guests to bring guests to their rooms' ('Not the Kind of Press,' 2012). Informal networks offer online information to men seeking to visit the city for sex (Puello Sarabia and Ardila Palacio, 2019).

Procurers sell children to US tourists for sexual purposes in the offshore Rosario islands (Bedoya, 2014; Montaño, 2018).[11] A renowned figure known locally as 'Madame' spent much of the past decade in an alliance with Israelis, shepherding children around the historic center of the city in search of tourists, and organizing hotel, beach, yacht, and island sex parties with 250 female workers from Cartagena and Venezuela (all 14–17 years old). Local officials were bribed and girls dispatched to the Bahamas and Miami. Hundreds of Israeli soldiers were regular customers (Montaño, 2018; Charles, 2018). The link between the military and such activities is longstanding: the development of sex tourism for US nationals, for instance, accelerated with participation by soldiers fighting in Việt Nam (Boyer, 2002). This takes us to a more overt and glamorous sex tourist: 007.

James Bond

A frogman emerges from Cuban waters. He kills a guard, enters a factory, sets explosives, and departs. Stripping down from his scuba gear, we see he is dressed in formal summer evening wear. Pausing only to adjust an adorning flower, he saunters into a cantina and awaits the explosion he has set. It's 1964, it's *Goldfinger* (dir. Guy Hamilton), and Sean Connery *is* James Bond, probably the single most violent and lasting male in cultural history after God.

Espionage involves surreptitiously conveying information about a country, company, or union to its enemy or rival. It is typified by theft, secrecy, trust, and lies. Loyalty, patriotism, and the mundanity of public employment are reforged as plays with death, doom, and style. The mystery of espionage fiction usually concerns enemy plans, allies, and methods—schemes devised by a geopolitical opponent that are foiled in the lonely hour of the last instance by a lone operative, thanks to superior beauty, physique, ingenuity, and technology. One might regard the genre as part of obtaining Gramscian consent, because it glamorizes the work of spies as entertainment, patriotism, and raison d'état. Bond's image as an unquestioningly loyal Englishman, serial philanderer, gadget man, and fanatic for the high life appears to fit Connell's analysis.

Eco identified these narrative structures in Ian Fleming's novels: MI6 chief 'M' subdues Bond, the villain subdues the woman, even if Bond seems to have converted and protected her, capitalism subdues state socialism, white Britain subdues other racial groups, death subdues love, and moderation subdues excess. This series of contests takes place as follows: 'M' assigns a task to Bond; a villain or his agents appear to 007; he does battle with them; a woman appears to Bond, who seduces her; the villain captures 007 and sometimes the woman, then tortures his captives; Bond kills the villain and/or his perversely proportioned assistant; and 007 escapes to temporary happiness with the woman, who is then taken from him (Eco, 1966: 156). These sequences vary in order and frequency, but the pattern is clear.

Eco proposes 14 pairs to each narrative. The first six are as follows: Bond and M, Bond and the villain, the villain and the woman, the woman and Bond, the free world and the Soviet Union, and Britain and non-Anglo-Saxon countries. The above are all about relationships between actants. The next eight binary opposites pair human tendencies and experiences: duty and sacrifice, cupidity and ideals, love and death, chance and planning, luxury and discomfort, excess and moderation, perversion and innocence, and loyalty and disloyalty (1966: 147). These apparent opposites merge in conflicts that demonstrate how each side of the pair is logocentrically dependent on its other. Race, sex, and international relations jumble together in a violent statism and individualism.

The Bond books and films are routinely held up as significant contributors to, and symptoms of, imperialism, sexism, Orientalism, class hierarchy, and jingoism; even as the first form of mass pornography (Baron, 1994: 69–70; Bold, 1993; Drummond, 1986: 66–67; Denning, 1992: 225). Theodore Roszak regarded 007 as the embodiment of technocracy, maintaining a 'clinical cool while dealing out prodigious sex or sadistic violence' (1969: 216). Ralph Miliband wryly remarked that Bond was one of the quintessential 'paragons of anti-Communist virtues' (1969: 226). John le Carré called him an 'international gangster' lacking 'all political context' (*Intimations*, 1966). Penelope Gilliatt worried that the films' 'brutal flippancy' was 'a new voice of the age' (1963). For Stuart Hall, Bond villains represented a casual yet marked and purposive racism (2010: 303). And looking back on 007's first half century on film, Jane Martinson said feminists were 'sick of a long-running multibillion-pound franchise that left a series of beautiful women as little more than roadkill in the path of the spy we never loved' (2012). Content analysis of the franchise's first 22 films discloses a doubling in the amount of violence over their 45 years (McAnally *et al.*, 2013).

Reactionary critics see things differently. Ayn Rand adored the 007 books for what she saw as their unabashed Romanticism and heroic transcendence (1975). Vincent Canby admired this 'steadfast agent for the military-industrial complex, a friend to the C.I.A. and a triumphant sexist' (1971). The *New York Times* published a 1998 piece on US covert action about using 'the black arts of sabotage and subversion to accomplish what diplomats and generals cannot.' The headline read 'James Bond vs. Saddam Hussein.' Latter-day fellow travelers lament that the US is not a nation of Bonds.

Breitbart is relieved that 007 can 'survive a miserable trend of male femi-nization' (Meyers, 2014) but horrified by 'the truly awful idea of a female or gay James Bond' and the recent films' 'anti-male stridency' (Nolte, 2019a, 2019b). The *American Conservative* luxuriates that 'Bond's Britain is relevant, wealthy, and influential, still a beacon of Western ingenuity,' regretting that 'today's man, coerced into believing in his own emascula-tion, would introduce himself to a lesbian named Pussy Galore by saying: "I respect your lifestyle choice." When James Bond met a lesbian named Pussy Galore, he slept with her' (Tippins, 2012).

In explaining 'Why James Bond Should Never Be a Woman,' the *Feder-alist* glorifies 007 as 'the quintessential alpha male' who 'is all about guard-ing the perimeter and protecting the group' deeming it 'exhilarating for a woman to bring the alpha male to his knees through her feminine wiles.' This is apparently 'the height of eroticism' (McAllister, 2017). The maga-zine is horrified by the prospect of what it calls 'a lefty's dream and a Bond fan's nightmare: a female-helmed James Bond' (Enck, 2019), preferring hypermasculine 'decisiveness, his willingness to take a life without remorse in the cause of queen and country' (Tracinski, 2015). The *Telegraph* lauds Bond as 'masculinity's last Hollywood outpost' (Daubney, 2015), while the *Daily Mail* avows that '007 may be a sexist dinosaur, but I still prefer it when a granite-tough alpha male saves the world' (Epstein, 2017). Producer Albert Broccoli called the films 'sadism for the family' (quoted in Barnes and Hearn, 1998: 20).

In 2001, the US military boasted to National Public Radio that it had created the latest generation of combat vehicles by sitting design engineers down to watch the film series for inspiration (Judd, 2001). MI6 reportedly delights in the franchise's free advertising, which assists in recruitment (Cain, 2019), while the CIA has a venture-capital fund known as In-Q-Tel, its title a homage to 007's quartermaster 'Q' (Keefe, 2010: 299).[12]

But Bond is truly contradictory. Amid the service to monarchy and nation, he is also lamentation incarnate, a last best hope—nostalgia for lost colonial power. The books' grief over the advent of a welfare state and the decline of empire is evident and profound (Bennett and Woollacott, 1987). Rand was troubled that the film franchise was laced with 'humor intended to undercut Bond's stature, to make him ridiculous' (1975). Her concerns were in keep-ing with Fleming's sorrow at the passing of 'real' heroism (Hellman, 1962). Meanwhile, the Vatican City's *L'Osservatore Romano* discerned 'a danger-ous mixture of violence, vulgarity, sadism and sex' in the series (quoted in 'Church Says,' 1965). And when the head of MI6 was played by a woman in Judi Dench, this was too much for reactionary critics. *TV Guide* called her a 'steely schoolmarm' whom no one would think of as 'den mother, unless the den were in Sparta' (McDonagh, 1995). For *Empire*, she was 'gruff'

(Newman, 2000), while *Time* derided her 'butch hairdo' and 'brusque Thatcherite manner' (Schickel, 1995). The *San Francisco Chronicle* was equally alarmed to find her 'butch-looking' (Stack, 1995), and *Variety* dismissed her as 'an iron maiden' (McCarthy, 1995).

Frequently a stricken figure, Bond's emotions are intense, his drinking dipsomaniacal, and his body routinely reduced. In conversation with Chandler, Fleming disclosed that he thought of 007 as a 'blunt instrument . . . he's always referred to as my hero. I don't see him as a hero myself. On the whole I think he's a rather unattractive man' (Fleming and Chandler, 2014: 31). Eric Hobsbawm saw Bond and his kind as 'compensating for their country's decline' (1995: 228). Rather wonderfully, Blofeld tells 007 in *Diamonds Are Forever* (dir. Guy Hamilton, 1971), 'Your pitiful little island hasn't even been threatened.'

The novels are laden with shocking scenes in which he is tortured (Adams, 2017). In *Casino Royale*, Le Chiffre uses 'a three-foot-long carpet-beater in twisted cane.' The details are enumerated in three pages of purple Fleming prose that describe the evil mastermind making his way across 007's 'sensitive part.' Bond awaited 'a wonderful period of warmth and langour leading into a sort of sexual twilight where pain turned to pleasure and where hatred and fear of the torturers turned to a masochistic infatuation' (1966: 119–22). This is one of the few scenes of torture from the novels that is reprised on film, complete with testicle-crushing sado-masochism (*Casino Royale*, dir. Martin Campbell, 2006).[13] That is also the film in which Dench's M echoes Fleming: she dismisses 007 as 'a blunt instrument.' In *Goldeneye* (dir. Martin Campbell, 1995), she had chided him as 'a sexist, misogynist dinosaur. A relic of the Cold War, whose boyish charms [are] wasted on me.'

His body—so often both shaken *and* stirred, by people, technologies, and events beyond its ken—is a perilous means of being known and of losing authority, a site of the potentially abject that must be objectified as a sign of self-control and autotelic satisfaction. Its stark movements between patriarchal power and limp failure embody the long crisis of a seemingly victorious Atlantic masculinity that began in 1945 with soldiers' return from the front to a crumbling economy and empire in Britain and new gender relations in the US, occasioned by the wartime economic mobilization of women followed by peacetime's suburbanization to discipline/reward the population.

Bond has always been a sign of the end of British confidence and a display of indignant but fated masculinity. By turns weak and strong, flaccid and erect, commonwealth and imperial, institutionalized and autonomous, 007 is always ready to be caddishly violent. This is nostalgia for lost colonialism; dismay at its decayed vestiges; signage of cultural imperialism; and a marker of ridiculous masculinity.

Conclusion

Reactionary writers, both female and male, celebrate what they take to be a laudable masculine power impelling Bond on in his romantic and imperial adventures, even through duels with his father figure 'M.' That propels us back to Machiavelli and knightly masculinity. The fact that 007 executes the will of a country listening desperately for echoes of a lost world domination is a reminder of Britain's geopolitical fallibility and desire to service US interests. But these are no mere fictional or parochial tendencies, as the hegemonic masculinity thesis shows with reference to sports and Latin America. For driving through all those stories is the complex phenomenon of nationalism.

Notes

1 https://operations.nfl.com/the-players/development-pipeline/nfl-rookie-transition-program/.
2 https://operations.nfl.com/the-players/evolution-of-the-nfl-player/.
3 www.armedforcesbowl.com/.
4 www.armedforcesbowl.com/great-american-patriot-award.
5 http://leanos.net/portfolio/intellectual-freedom-and-pat-tillman/.
6 http://colombiadiversa.org/base-datos/nacional/.
7 http://ethics.unwto.org/content/world-tourism-network-child-protection.
8 https://fundacionrenacer.org/.
9 https://www.icbf.gov.co/.
10 www.icbf.gov.co/portal/page/portal/PortalICBF/macroprocesos/misionales/restablecimiento/2/LM11.MPM5.P1%20Poblacion%20Especial%20Violencia%20Sexual%20v1.pdf.
11 www.youtube.com/watch?v=fuvMQAYhf48.
12 www.iqt.org/home-fall-2018/.
13 www.youtube.com/watch?v=mCNN2CnCAww.

4 Nation-state

Walter Scott's poem 'The Lay of the Last Minstrel' expresses the romantic, emotional tie that supposedly impels all worthy folk to fight for their homeland:

> Breathes there the man, with soul so dead,
> Who never to himself hath said,
> This is my own, my native land!
> Whose heart hath ne'er within him burn'd,
> As home his footsteps he hath turn'd,
> From wandering on a foreign strand!
> If such there breathe, go, mark him well;
> For him no Minstrel raptures swell;
> High though his titles, proud his name,
> Boundless his wealth as wish can claim;
> Despite those titles, power, and pelf,
> The wretch, concentred all in self,
> Living, shall forfeit fair renown,
> And, doubly dying, shall go down
> To the vile dust, from whence he sprung,
> Unwept, unhonor'd, and unsung.
>
> (1805)

Such warning sentiments about cosmopolitanism equating to selfishness are very ugly indeed. Think of UK Prime Minister Theresa May's (2017) insult, 'If you believe you're a citizen of the world, you're a citizen of nowhere. You don't understand what the very word "citizenship" means'; or Stalin referring to Jewish folks as 'rootless cosmopolitans' because he regarded international cultural consciousness and identification as inimical to Leninism (1946).

Or consider national anthems. 'La Marseillaise' is a notoriously blood-thirsty paean to racism and war: 'Qu'un sang impur/Abreuve nos sillons' (Let impure blood/Water our furrows). Colombians sing along to words glorifying the fact that their land emerged from 'surcos de dolores' (fur-rows of pain) and 'se baña en sangre de héroes' (is bathed in the blood of heroes). US citizens rise as one to celebrate weapons of mass destruction: 'the rocket's red glare, the bombs bursting in air . . . conquer we must, when our cause it is just.'[1] Chilean nationalists sing:

> Ha cesado, la lucha sangrienta
> ya es hermano, el que ayer opresor;
> del vasallo borramos la afrenta,
> combatiendo en el campo de honor[2]
> [The bloody fight has ended
> The former oppressor is now a brother;
> We have erased the insult,
> Fighting on the field of honor]

Mexicans luxuriate in their own bloodbath:

> Mexicanos, al grito de guerra
> El acero aprestad y el bridón;
> Y retiemble en sus centros la tierra
> Al sonoro rugir del cañón
> [Mexicans, at the cry of battle
> Lend your sword and bridle;
> The earth will tremble to its core
> At the cannon's roar][3]

Machiavelli invokes such sentiments to insist that:

> where the very safety of the country depends upon the resolution to be taken, no considerations of justice or injustice, humanity or cruelty, nor of glory or shame, should be allowed to prevail. But putting all other considerations aside, the only question should be, What course will save the life and liberty of the country?
>
> (1950: 528)

These words undergird raison d'état. In accepting the Nobel Prize for Lit-erature, Harold Pinter told this 1980s story about a delegation led by Father John Metcalf opposing US aid to the Nicaraguan *Contras* that met with the State Department's Ray Seitz:

Father Metcalf said: 'Sir, I am in charge of a parish in the north of Nicaragua . . . a Contra force attacked the parish. They destroyed everything . . . raped nurses and teachers, slaughtered doctors.' . . . Seitz . . . spoke with some gravity. 'Father,' he said, 'let me tell you something. In war, innocent people always suffer.'

(Pinter 2009: 479–80)

At other times, nationalistic sentiments are simply incanted, without more meaning than the requirement to conform. As a ten-year old, Eco knew the essentials of survival under fascism:

I received the First Provincial Award of Ludi Juveniles (a voluntary, compulsory competition for young Italian Fascists—that is, for every young Italian). I elaborated with rhetorical skill on the subject 'Should we die for the glory of Mussolini and the immortal destiny of Italy?' My answer was positive. I was a smart boy.

(1995)

And acts of bloody nationalism may arise from the self-deception of instrumental reasoning. Robert Oppenheimer, who led the murderous Manhattan Project, testified to the US Atomic Energy Commission (1954) during the Cold War about the instrumental rationality that animated those who created its terrifying technology. Many of these scientists were progressives. But once they saw a bomb was feasible, its inevitable impact on the Earth's inhabitants lost intellectual and emotional significance for them. Such considerations were overtaken by what he termed the project's

technically sweet quality: . . . when you see something that is technically sweet, you go ahead and do it and you argue about what to do about it only after you have had your technical success. That is the way it was with the atomic bomb.

After September 11, 2001, Robert Bellah queried the Second World War as a justification for US and British atrocities then and since. He asked: 'is it so entirely clear that we won?' By which he meant, not the military struggle, but 'the extent that we became like the enemy we opposed.' Bellah was concentrating on the way that early condemnations of the Germans for targeting civilians were displaced by Allied attacks of just that kind, from bombing Dresden, Hamburg, and Tokyo to the nuclear holocausts visited on Hiroshima and Nagasaki (2002: 255).

There is a famous story about the head of the Royal Air Force's Bomber Command during the war, Arthur Harris (popularly known as 'Bomber,' but referred to by his subordinates as 'Butcher'). Harris was being driven at speed to London. A police officer pulled the car over and said: 'You could have killed someone.' His reply? 'Young man, I kill thousands of people every night' (quoted in Wilkins, 2020). The decision to engage in urban bombing was not just a reaction to the Blitz; it also responded to the Butt Report (Bensusan-Butt, 1941), which demonstrated the failure of bombing Germany's military and industrial sites. Despite constant denials, Bomber Command decided to target non-combatants via blanket assaults on cities as a form of terror.

The genealogy from urban bombing to latter-day US mass killing and undercover adventurism is apt. Throughout the Cold War and since, the United States has undermined democratic and/or socialist governments, notably via a campaign of mass murders by CIA operatives during the American War in Việt Nam and the assassinations of Dominican Republic President Rafael Trujillo and Patrice Lumumba, leader of the Congo, in the early 1960s. When Allende was selected as the socialist candidate for the Chilean presidency, the Nixon administration secretly instigated strikes by truck drivers to obstruct commerce. When he was elected in 1970, it decided to 'make the economy scream,' to use a notorious CIA expression of the time. This policy saw the US ambassador undertake that 'not a nut or bolt will be allowed to reach Chile under Allende,' via a combination of public and corporate money. The director of the CIA perjured himself before Congress over agency support for the 1973 coup against Allende. After pleading no contest in a subsequent trial, he waited a few years, then received a public commendation from Reagan for services to the public. Reagan's administration sought to assassinate Libyan President Gaddafi. It bombed Nicaraguan power plants and mined port facilities as part of its illegal covert operations against the Sandinistas, which may also have included staging a faux Nicaraguan commando raid on El Salvador in 1982 to create a casus belli on behalf of the latter's brutal dictatorship. The CIA gave the *Contras* a kidnapping, terrorism, and blackmail manual, the infamous *Operaciones Sicológicas en Guerra de Guerrillas* (Psychological Operations in Guerrilla Warfare) (officials quoted in Johnson, 1996: 169; Jeffreys-Jones, 1989: 183, 238–39; Cockburn and St. Clair, 1998: 98–101, 107–08; Polmar and Allen, 1997: 257–58).

In keeping with these *aperçus*, after some theoretical work, this chapter will look at the promise of cosmopolitanism and citizenship, the nature of the state, and the horror of war.

Nationalism

The 1919 Treaty of Versailles concluded the First World War. The victorious powers regarded national self-determination (apart from freedom for their own 'possessions') as the best route to peace, along with open markets and a system of international governance that would control the warlike tendencies of the vanquished and others. But imperialism was not dismantled, and when the Depression hit, the immediate response was restrictive trade practices, such as tariffs and other barriers. Alongside the emergence of fascist nationalism, it produced the conditions of possibility for the Second World War (Strange, 1979). The idea of nations as guarantors of peace was compromised by the victors protecting their own empires, then distorting the trading system because of an enormous economic crisis.

Meanwhile, the ideology of nationalism, always close to doctrines of autochthony, autarky, and autarchy, was used by emergent great powers (the USSR, Japan, Germany, and Italy) to justify political or racial superiority in much the same way as French and British imperialists. Although the claims and efforts of ethno-nationalists frequently failed to override more universal ideas promulgated through religion, democracy, and human rights (Horkheimer, 2013), where the bourgeoisie failed to adopt comprehensively liberal ideas, and technological connections across borders were countered by local demagoguery, collective ideas of superiority and destiny found fecund fields. A refusal to identify with humanity as a whole was at the core of such nationalism (Adorno, 1997, 2007; Adorno *et al.*, 1950).

One tradition, populated by conservative ethno-nationalists, argues that nations are constants across history, albeit changing their morphology with time and circumstance (Herder, 2002). They are sustained through supposedly indelible ties: origin myths, languages, customs, races, and religions (Smith, 2000). This position is exemplified by Scott's poem mentioned at the beginning of this chapter. For those more in thrall to modernity, such claims are invented traditions (Hobsbawm and Ranger, 2002). Far from being the outcome of abiding mythologies, the materiality and idea of the nation derived from the Industrial Revolution, which brought places together that had not previously been linked. Relatively isolated subsistence villages were transformed through the interdependence engendered by capitalist organizations, the commodification of everyday relations, and the sense of unity generated from nation-binding technologies and institutions, most notably print and public education (Gellner, 1988).

Even as the nation is manufactured, it is said to be an already extant, authentic essence of statehood and personhood. The state articulates the nation as a spirit-in-dwelling, which gives it legitimacy, for nations are coterminous with systems of government. Hence William Morris's lament for the museum as a seemingly peaceful monument to artifactual knowledge sustained by the state but really 'a tale of violence, destruction, and carelessness, as its treasured scraps tell us' (1978: 506). Wander through the British Museum and see travelers of every background pointing with fascination and admiration at relics of plunder and killing, of imperial lust.

Much of world tourism relies on commodifying and governing a heritage of violence and war (Lisle, 2016; Ojeda, 2013).

As the first half of 'nation-state' suggests, there is a cultural component to the couplet—an element of belonging, identification, ideology, hegemony, commitment. This is the ideological state apparatus, of schooling, propaganda, patriotism, imperialism, religion, and xenophobia (Althusser, 1977). As Schumpeter put it, nationalism 'satisfies the need for surrender to a concrete and familiar super-personal cause, the need for self-glorification and violent self-assertion' (1966: 12).

The second half of the name refers not only to these organs of sanctioned violence and social control, but also to politics, policy, administration, and justice, to be covered in greater detail below. So the national legacy underpinning the United States is a 19th-century regime of clearance, genocide, and enslavement as much as democracy; a modernity built, as each successful one has been, on brutality:

> The property owners of the modern world are not the legitimate heirs of Lockean individuals . . . they are the inheritors of those who, for example, stole, and used violence to steal the common lands of England from the common people, vast tracts of North America from the American Indian, much of Ireland from the Irish, and Prussia from the original non-German Prussians.
>
> (Macintyre, 2007: 251)

There is another history, of longing for self-determination and resisting imperialism. The nation has been a core resistive concept of decolonization, providing a means of registering claims for inclusion in both narratives and institutions (Cabral, 1973)—a veritable font of resistance to imperial suzerainty. Nkrumah (1969: 88) avowed that 'nationalism is the ideological channel of the anti-colonialist struggle' and Lyotard viewed it as a key response to 'the profound *desocialization* produced by imperialism' (1993: 238). Du Bois spoke of the 'personal apostles of African nationalism, who wander across the vast distances of Africa and talk with the people' (1942: 72).

In general, however, nationalism is rightly damned for its maleness, brutality, warmongering, and other failings: Luxemburg (1986: 331) spoke for many when she denounced 'the empty wordiness of nationalism as an instrument of bourgeois domination.' The absurdity of nationalism is not confined to the right, for the specter of Stalin is never far behind: 'the whole, disastrous experience of "state socialism" which came to so abrupt and dramatic an end in 1989' has meant that 'the entire historical basis and trajectory of "the left" in serious politics has had to be rethought' (Hall,

1995: 25–26). Its legacy is a twin horror, of 'violence and waste' (Said, 1994: 26), violence against land and people and waste of resources, both natural and human—on all sides.

Vast numbers of US citizens imagine that the military embodies their essence, whereas government is their enemy—little realizing that the state is nowhere more present than in its repressive apparatus, also known as the police, army, and so on, entities 'whose 'civilizing' mission never ceases to be glorified' (Poulantzas, 2008: 321; Althusser, 1977). This is what Mead referred to when he suggested that war's capacity to bring people together within a national frame could override every other distinction between them, endowing patriots with the strongest sense of self imaginable—one dedicated to the defeat of others (2011: 278). Such a seemingly superordinate claim on identity is a problem, for 'violence is promoted by the cultivation of a sense of inevitability about some allegedly unique—often belligerent—identity that we are supposed to have and which apparently makes extensive demands on us' (Sen, 2006: 27). So the identities of loving parent, belligerent baseball fan, cricketing tragic, poor lover, voracious reader, *Friends* (1994–2004) fanatic, or judgmental vegan are subordinated, as if they did not truly become us next to this ultimate identification. In Kristeva's words:

> When exposed to violence, individuals despair of their own qualities, undervalue their achievements and yearnings, run down their own freedoms whose preservation leaves so much to chance; and so they withdraw into a sullen, warm private world, unnamable and biological, the impregnable 'aloofness' of a weird primal paradise—family, ethnicity, nation, race.
>
> (1993: 3)

Such things happen at moments of geopolitical rupture, when switching points disclose rusted cores: Yugoslavia becoming Serb versus Bosnian, or partition pitting Muslim against Hindu, when demagoguery denies prior cohabitation in the name of a purported essence. This is what Eric Wolf termed 'the identity politics of the state' (2010: 39).

The state

Democracy is conventionally said to arise and thrive in the interactions of governments and populations, its models being the French and American Revolutions. But Machiavelli's maxims remain relevant: even rulers who wish 'to make a profession of goodness' must 'learn how not to be good' (1950: 56). Recall Weber's very definition of sovereignty as a 'human community that (successfully) claims the monopoly of the legitimate use of physical force within a given territory' (1946). That places violence at the center of statehood.

In trying to understand the Communist Manifesto's only rival as the most destructive and instructive fetish of modernity, also known as the US Constitution, Lippmann interpreted the document as a means of creating a white, male, property-owning civil society that would stop killing indiscriminately (i.e., among its own). Here's what he came up with:

> Without civil organization the people are at one time a helpless crowd, at another a horde trampling all before them; then they are mobs which destroy each other; then isolated individuals, each man against all the others . . . until again, in the cycle of their impotent violence, they become a horde led by a master of the crowd.
>
> (1982: 23)

Those fears compel not only the immense reserve power of the state—its capacity to draw on unimagined authority to describe, categorize, and stigmatize its population—but also its intimate imbrication with theories of personhood, of the kind mentioned in Chapter 2. They are incarnate in the psy-function, religion, and ideology.

For Bertrand Russell, a lock on violence was the 'essence of government.' This was legitimate, provided that its sole purpose was 'to diminish the total amount of force used in the world' (2009: 36–37). C. Wright Mills argued that 'the threat of violence' represented 'the coercive power always present in decisive political questions' (1963: 305). Wittfogel agreed that

> all governments deserving the name have ways of imposing their will on their subjects, and the use of violence is always among them. But different societies develop different patterns of integrating (or fragmenting) violence and of controlling (or not controlling) it.
>
> (1967: 139)

Morgenthau's realist theory of international relations held that conflicts of all kinds were generally resolved on terms most favorable to states with the strongest military. He, too, maintained that the domestic 'threat of political violence' via the police, prison, execution, or war was 'an intrinsic element of politics' (1948: 13). Lenin deemed the state 'a special organization of force . . . an organization of violence for the suppression of some class' (2014: 61). For Negri,

> founded upon the dissolution of natural relations and the alienation of the indefinite desire for power (puissance) of individuals, the political

institution of sovereignty invents Right as its own principle, thereby guaranteeing civil peace.

(Alliez and Negri, 2003: 110)

Achille Mbembe argues that 'necropolitics' is the state's fundamental form of life, 'that the ultimate expression of sovereignty resides, to a large degree, in the power and capacity to dictate who may live and who must die' (2003: 11).

Such critics are of course dependent on Tolstoy's provocation that 'government is violence' (1990). And they must recognize that this ideology relies on some level of acceptance by the citizenry—that they might one day need the police, that people are often beastly, that other governments may covet the territory where they live. This became a fundamental aspect of modernity: 'when one confronts the fear of early and violent death, one becomes willing to regulate oneself and to accept external regulations that will secure life against its dangers' (Connolly, 1993: 29). Hence Hobbes extolling some level of protection against the 'danger of violent death; and the life of man, solitary, poor, nasty, brutish, and Short' (1651: 78) and Hegel disparaging the 'savage state of life' as 'marked by brutal passions and deeds of violence' (2001: 56). This 'state of Nature' is characterized by 'injustice and violence, of untamed natural impulses' (2001: 57).

Even as revolutionary France was embarking on a regime of slaughter, public health campaigns were underway in an ongoing Janus-faced 'game between death and life' (Foucault, 1991b: 4). Out of that came the following prospect: 'Maybe what is really important for our modernity—that is, for our present—is not so much the étatisation of society, as the governmentalization of the state' (Foucault, 1991a: 103).

In 18th-century Europe, the government of territory became secondary to the government of things and social relations. Biopower freed the arts of government from the pre-modern motifs and idées fixes of the sovereign and the household. The population displaced the prince as a site for accumulating power, and the home was displaced by the economy as a newly anthropomorphized and international dynamic of social intervention and achievement. The populace became the province of statistics, and the nation was bounded not by the direct exertion of juridical influence or domestic authority, but by forms of knowledge that granted 'the people' life. The epidemic and the map supplemented the kitchen and church (Foucault, 1991a: 98–99).

Government was conceived and actualized in terms of climate, disease, industry, finance, custom, and disaster—literally, a concern with life and death and what could be calculated and managed between them. Wealth and health became goals to be attained through the disposition of capacities across the population: 'biological existence was reflected in political existence.' This biopower brought 'life and its mechanisms into the realm of explicit calculations' and made 'knowledge-power an agent of transformation of human life.' Bodies were identified with politics because managing them was part of running countries and empires, with 'the life of the species . . . wagered on its own political strategies' (Foucault, 1991a: 92–95, 97; 1978a: 143).

Governing people came to mean, most centrally and critically, obeying the 'imperative of health: at once the duty of each and the objective of all' (Foucault, 1991b: 277). Capitalism was articulated to the state's desire to deliver a docile and healthy labor force to business; but not only to business, and not merely in a way that showed the lineage of that desire. Cholera, sanitation, and prostitution were figured as problems for governments to address through 'the emergence of the health and physical well-being of the population in general as one of the essential objectives of political power.' In shifting its tasks from naked, controlling power to generative, productive power, government in general increasingly aimed to '"make" live and "let" die,' as well as 'take life or let live' (Foucault, 2003b: 241). Biopower subjected bodies to regulation, self-surveillance, and self-discipline, initiated in asyla, hospitals, prisons, schools, and plantations. It made the relationship of populations to their environments a central strut of governance in 18th- and 19th-century Europe, as productivity and health were linked to climatic and geographic surroundings. Each element was subject to human intervention and hence governmental interest, via forecasts, measurements, and estimates (2004: 245).

But the thinness of interpersonal and social peace is forever lurking, and nowhere better expressed than by Mannheim:

> Democratic society always lives under the shadow of possible disorder and chaos, since in principle all social units have a claim to assert themselves and there is no certainty that they will compromise their divergent interests and aspirations before their conflict becomes acute and violent. The democratized individual, too, is constantly aware of chaos lurking in the depths of his own personality. There is no pre-existent pattern of order guaranteed for ever in a democratic world.
>
> (2017: 473)

Unger's three forms of life for the state—the ability to transform life through equality and education, to operate in partnership in society via democracy, and to wage war against that very society through oppression—are in constant negotiation (1987: 93).

While the idea of a state monopoly may have been compromised by the omniscient interests of vicious god-botherers and greedy capitalists (Brown, 2010), government remains their goal and tool, respectively (Strange, 1998). Utopian adherents of capitalism celebrate the triumph of the market as a purportedly demotic, non-bureaucratic expression of popular sentiment. Dystopians see a world dominated by unaccountable consumerism and religious spectacle (Falk, 2004: 21). Polanyi explained that 'the market has been the outcome of a conscious and often violent intervention on the part of government which imposed the market organization on society' (2001: 258).

In terms of geopolitics, the world has been contoured by the earth-shattering concatenation of political-economic events since the 18th century:

- the shift from absolute monarchy to parliamentary democracy;
- the social upheavals of imperialism, colonialism, slavery, war, postcolonialism, industrialization, urbanization, human rights, feminism, and climate change; and
- the expansion of global capitalism

The coordinates for those transformations derive from four key events: the Treaties of Tordesillas in 1494 and Westphalia in 1648 and the Washington and Berlin Conferences of 1884. Tordesillas acknowledged the emergence of empire, as the pope mediated rivalries between Spain and Portugal through a bifurcation of the world—the first recorded conceptualization of the globe as a site of conquest and exploitation. Westphalia instantiated sovereign control of territory for European nations. Washington standardized Greenwich as the axis of time and cartography, the same year as Africa was divided by imperialists at Berlin (Schaeffer, 1997). These developments effectively marked out the world as a site of interconnected government and commerce, with Western Europe and the US its domineering epicenter.

Capitalism's uneven, unequal development has paralleled that violent cartography. Mercantilist accumulation and imperialism from 1500 to 1800 were followed by the classical era of capital and its Industrial Revolution, founded on the use of natural resources for manufacturing copper, steel, and fuel. Northern industrial development and agrarian change were partnered by European migration to the Americas (to deal with population overflow) and the division of Africa and Asia (delivering raw materials and enslaved labor) (Amin, 1997; Reich, 1999).

Race has been a crucial index and cause of such violence. Bolívar thought of the 'new' Americans as bicultural products of usurping Spaniards and resistant indigenous folk, and hence inheritors of both a rule-governed struggle to impose empire and a fiercely elemental refusal of invasion and conquest (Villota Galeano, 2017). The reality was that the violence of the *conquista* (conqueror) amplified following independence, as *criollo* (locally born 'Spanish') rulers sought to take over and exploit territory to confirm their statehood and economic future (Colmenares, 1996). Elsewhere, 'regimes of violence imposed upon slave and ex-slave populations, in the case of the United States, were not separate and apart from the general workings of local, state, and federal government' but integral to them, as the backlash against civil-rights campaigning made all too apparent (Hanchard, 2018: 256).

Orwell looked back guiltily on his time as a colonial police officer:

> It was a double oppression that we were committing. Not only were we hanging people and putting them in jail and so forth; we were doing it in the capacity of unwanted foreign invaders. The Burmese themselves never really recognized our jurisdiction. The thief whom we put in prison did not think of himself as a criminal justly punished, he thought of himself as the victim of a foreign conqueror.
>
> (1958: 73)

And the mythology associated with all forms of imperialism remains powerful, courtesy generations of thinkers, both popular and otherwise, in thrall to its power:

> Rather than affirming the interdependence of various histories on one another and the necessary interaction of contemporary societies with one another, the rhetorical separation of cultures assured a murderous imperial contest between them—the sorry tale is repeated again and again.
>
> (Said, 1994: 38)

The targets in Cold War struggles by proxy were Latin America and new African and Asian states emerging from imperial control, which were seen as potentially drawn to Marxist-Leninist-Maoist ideas if they were not shown the one true path to life, liberty, and the pursuit of cornflakes. Former colonial powers and the United States told the rest of the world to instill nationalist fellow feeling and individual/state sovereignty as habits of thought in order to become viable independent states. The daily prayer called for a 'modern individual' who would not fall for socialist temptations. Development necessitated the displacement of 'the particularistic norms' of tradition by 'more universalistic' blends of the modern, as part of the creation of an 'achievement-oriented' society (Pye, 1965: 19).

Apart from their unreconstructed narcissism, these precepts disavowed the existing international division of labor and the success of imperial and commercial powers in annexing states and/or their labor forces. Although later modernization models were more sensitive to conflicts over wealth, influence, and status, they did not measure up to critical theories of dependent development, underdevelopment, unequal exchange, world-systems history, center-periphery relations, and cultural and media imperialism. These radical critiques of capitalist modernization shared the view that the transfer of technology, politics, and economics had become unattainable, because the emergence of multinational corporations united business and government to regulate cheap labor markets, produce new consumers, and guarantee pliant regimes (Reeves, 1993: 24–25, 30).

Since the Cold War, it has been argued that we are witnessing 'the contemporary unpicking of the so-called Westphalian model of territorial states that monopolize violent resources' (Keane, 2004: 179) both in terms of the impunity of violent actors and the failure to deliver basic social services to citizens. Habermas says de-territorialized terrorism, by non-state as well as state actors, has been unleashed by a potent mixture of faith, fraud, ethnicity, and economics in response to Western violence, taunts, and fiefdoms (2006). When combined with imperialism and colonialism, these forces produced the contemporary map of the world as a contingent, violent outcome of invasion and independence, expressed in revolution, war, slavery, insurrection, national liberation, religious politics, militias, and standing armies.

Amy Chua has investigated the latter-day junction of democracy, neoliberalism, and ethnic-minority economic oligarchies: when wealthy minorities privileged by former colonial powers confront popular backlashes against their economic power via majoritarian rejection of cultural difference and economies enrich 'the market-dominant minority, democratization increases the political voice and power of the frustrated majority' (2003: 124). This is the conundrum 'that turns free market democracy into an engine of ethnic conflagration' (2003: 6). Class, corruption, and race jumble together, as 'market-dominant minorities, along with their foreign-investor partners, invariably come to control the crown jewels of the economy . . . oil in Russia and Venezuela, diamonds in South Africa, silver and tin in Bolivia, jade, teak, and rubies in Burma' (2003: 10). Free markets concentrate *wealth dis*proportionately, while democracies concentrate *politics pro*portionately. Political enfranchisement and its economic opposite are mediated through cultural difference, with the outcome revolutionary. The horrors of Rwanda in the 1990s illustrate what happens when ethno-nationalist populism draws on majority resentment to quash minority economic power, based on cultural difference (2003: 11–13, 16–17).

War

Few theorists of war have been transcended Clausewitz's capacious yet precise definition of it (Sharma, 2015), even if his use of the first-person plural is troubling in its certitude about the universal desire for power: 'War is . . . an act of force to compel our enemy to do our will' (1989: 75). He avowed that it 'is not merely an act of policy but a true political Instrument, a continuation of political intercourse, carried on with other means' (1989: 87).[4] In terms of when it is morally legitimate to make war, Walzer's classic account adopts the commonsense liberal position: 'resistance to armed aggression' that ends 'with the military defeat of the aggressor.' That becomes complicated when the very system of government that has been defeated is committed to genocide or imperialism. Losing a war does not end those desires, and hence the drive for fundamental political transformation following military success (2006: x–xii). So we find Garvey avowing support for war 'to free one's self or protect one's rights or heritage' (2004: pos. 614).

Hobbes argued that

> the causes of war and desolation proceed from those passions, by which we strive to accommodate ourselves, and to leave others as far as we can behind us: it followeth that that passion by which we strive mutually to accommodate each other, must be the cause of peace.
>
> (1640)

Explanations vary over time and space, albeit with some recurring aspects. Wars have been understood for centuries as 'an aberration in human affairs . . . an occurrence beyond rational control,' and more recently as effects of masculinity, class greed, or evolutionary necessity (Howard, 1984: 90). The political organization of the modern state since the 19th century has facilitated national mobilization for war in most parts of the world, while progress in armaments, if it can be called that, has done the same for individuals and non-state collective actors (Unger, 1987: 118).

Institutionalist political science lists as causes of war 'power theories, power transition theories, the relationship between economic interdependence and war, diversionary theories of conflict, domestic coalitional theories, and the nature of decision-making under risk and uncertainty' (Levy, 1998). Quantoid neoliberals advise that

> there are two prerequisites for a war between (rational) actors. One is that the costs of war cannot be overwhelmingly high . . . there must be some plausible situations in the eyes of the decision makers such that

the anticipated gains from a war in terms of resources, power, glory, territory, and so forth exceed the expected costs of conflict. . . .

Second, . . . there has to be a failure in bargaining . . . an inability to reach a mutually advantageous and enforceable agreement.

(Jackson and Morelli, 2011)

This decontextualized game theory, founded on rational action as defined by a capitalist consumer mentality, dominates the deracinated world of much social science—the reductive, selfish side of rationality (Altman, 2015; Meadwell, 2016). Psy-function explanations have been diminished to game-theoretical assumptions and their cozily artificial experiments (Böhm *et al.*, 2015). Cliometricians are also subject to the imposing spells of this warlockcraft (Eloranta, 2016; Jenke and Gelpi, 2017).

Such approaches form part of the warfare/welfare mentality that colors US and northern European social science, alongside service to capital. In the case of war, we see these forms of life adopted and encouraged by technocrats and militarists alike (Roxborough, 2015). In short, mainstream academia, diplomacy, and the military are wedded to the notion that 'war between states is to be seen in terms of rationally decided aggression rather than in the internationalization of social conflict' (Halliday, 1990: 207).

Contra those perspectives, we confront Hobson's ideas about imperialism being driven by the capitalist problem of over-production (1902); Marxist theories of class war caused by unequal control of the means of production; Maoist arguments for the peasantry as motors of revolutionary change; feminist critiques of masculine violence; and postcolonial insights into wars that derive from decolonizing cartography (Gruffydd Jones, 2006).

Keynes (1936: 376) provides a succinct political-economic explanation:

> War has several causes. Dictators and others such, to whom war offers, in expectation at least, a pleasurable excitement, find it easy to work on the natural bellicosity of their peoples. But, over and above this, facilitating their task of fanning the popular flame, are the economic causes of war, namely, the pressure of population and the competitive struggle for markets.

The development economist Frances Stewart (2002) advises that

- the incidence of war has been rising since 1950, mostly within rather than between states;
- wars may be prompted by race and religion, but with underlying economic causes; and

- the principal stimuli are political, economic, and social inequality; poverty; economic stagnation; poor government; high unemployment; environmental degradation; and individual incentives

The Royal Geographical Society nominates 'land disputes, politics, religious and cultural differences and the distribution and use of resources' as causes, while the Heidelberg Institute for International Conflict Research database finds that ideological struggle is a source of most wars, generally nested with other factors.[5]

A new kind of state violence began in the 1960s and has continued because of several factors:

- changes in the global division of labor, as manufacturing left the Global North and subsistence agriculture was eroded in the Global South
- demographic growth through unprecedented public-health initiatives
- increases in refugees following numerous conflicts among satellite states of the United States and the Soviet Union
- transformations of these struggles into intra- and transnational violence when half the imperial couplet unraveled
- the associated decline of state socialism and triumph of finance capital
- vastly augmented human trafficking
- the elevation of consumption as a site of social action and public policy
- renegotiation of the 1940s–70s compact across the West among capital, labor, and government, reversing that period's redistribution of wealth downward
- deregulation of key sectors of the economy
- the revival of Islam as a transnational religion and political project, and
- the development of civil-rights and social-movement discourses and institutions, extending cultural difference from tolerating the aberrant to querying the normal, and commodifying the result

The dilemmas that derive from these changes underpin John Gray's critique of 'the West's ruling myth . . . that modernity is a single condition, everywhere the same and always benign'—a veritable embrace of Enlightenment values. Modernity has as much to do with global financial deregulation, organized crime, and religious violence as it does with democracy, uplift, and opportunity, and it has just as much to do with neoliberalism, religion, and authoritarianism as it does with freedom, science, and justice (2003: 1–2, 46).

Running through all this, of course, is the technocracy of war. In his farewell speech as US president, Eisenhower memorably condemned 'the military-industrial complex' (1972). Its lust for power seemingly ever-growing, 'this coercive apparatus constitutes a vast, sprawling and resourceful establishment, whose professional leaders are men of high status and great influence inside the state system and in society' (Miliband, 1969: 52). In 2015, 39% of US income tax went to military institutions (The Peace Alliance, 2015).

There have been many outbursts of regressive nationalism, whether via the belligerence of the United States, the anti-immigrant stance of Western Europe, or crackdowns on minorities in Eastern Europe, Asia, and the Arab world (Halliday, 2004). The populist outcome is often violent, resulting in, for example, race riots in 30 British cities in the 1980s, pogroms against Roma and migrant workers in Germany in the 1990s and Spain in 2000, the intifadas, migrant-worker and youth struggles in France in 1990 and 2005, and so on. Virtually any arrival can be racialized, though particular feeling is often reserved for expatriates from former colonies (Downing and Husband, 2005: xi, 7). The two most important sites of migration from the Global South to the Global North—Turkey and Mexico—see state and vigilante violence alongside corporate embrace in host countries, while donor nations increasingly recognize the legitimacy of a hybrid approach to citizenship (Bauböck, 2005: 9).

Cosmopolitanism and citizenship

What of cosmopolitanism? A core Enlightenment ideal, cosmopolitanism suffered with the ongoing triumph of the state and nationalist ideology, but became au courant again due to the need for ways of living together in a globalizing economy with vast migration and cultural exchange. Its linguistic heritage blends universalism with particularism—an encounter between the cosmos and the citizen staged again and again since Aristotle, and frequently leading to a profound suspiciousness and doubt about one's loyalty (Benhabib, 2011), as per May and Stalin. This dialectic takes many forms: Burke (1774) addressing the electors of Bristol, Angela Davis (2003) calling for a new emancipation via the destruction of prisons, Jesus Christ teaching about universal equality, and Kant (2006) theorizing world citizenship.

The superpower concept was first enunciated in 1944, just as nuclear weaponry and the defeat of the Axis powers were on the horizon (Fox, 1944). Beyond the utopian rhetoric of global peace that was so derided by realists (Miller, 1981), classical theorists have argued for the success of a relatively ordered and peaceful world system since 1945 thanks to the strength of large states, their desire to eschew direct conflict with one another, and the emergence of a raft of international organizations operating beyond territories and armies (Bull, 2002). But Hobbes's position that the state can enforce the rule of law domestically but not internationally has remained a dominant argument in the case against world government as an unattainable goal (Falk, 2004: 7).

The histories of the League of Nations, the UN, the Organization of American States, the African Union, the Arab League, the Association of Southeast Asian Nations, and the European Union stand for the failure of world and even regional government. Less grandiose, more technical subgroups manage with reasonable success the international relations of postage, health, sports, telecommunications, and immigration. Those entities arose from a notion that the anarchic world of states could be governed in much the same way as individual countries managed their populations. But James Der Derian suggests we now live in a period of 'Antidiplomacy.' States conduct international affairs through 'a technostrategic triad of surveillance, terror, and speed' (1992: viii). Does contemporary citizenship offer a more positive future for cosmopolitanism?

The last 200 years of modernity have produced three zones of citizenship, with partially overlapping but also distinct historicities:

- the political (the right to reside and vote)
- the economic (the right to work and prosper)
- the cultural (the right to know and speak)

They correspond to the French Revolution's cry *'liberté, égalité, fraternité'* (liberty, equality, solidarity).

Classical political theory accorded representation to the citizen through the state. Political citizenship—*liberté*—emerged from the brutality of the English Revolution. It locates sovereignty in 'relations between the general will and its representative organs' (Foucault, 2003b: 152). For all its focus on the nation and the state, the founding assumption of political citizenship is that personal freedom is both the wellspring of good government *and* the source of its authority over individuals.

Political citizenship gives the right to vote, be represented in government, and enjoy physical security, in return for ceding violence to the state (the United States is contradictory about this issue, as we have seen). Despite its focus on nation and state, the founding assumption of political citizenship is that personal freedom is both the wellspring of good government *and* the source of its authority over individuals. In Aristotle's words, 'man [*sic*] is by nature a political animal,' who gathers with others to form a state for their mutual benefit (1963: 61). In Rousseau's paradox, this involves 'making men free by making them subject' (1975: 123).

The preconditions and functions of political citizenship are largely 'dependent on [the] internal development' of the sovereign states that emerged from the necessity to deal with European religious conflicts of the

16th and 17th centuries (Halliday, 2001: 86; Barry, 2001: 21). Ignoring the fact that citizenship was forged in relation to bellicose encounters of West and East, 19th- and early 20th-century liberal philosophers postulated it as the linkage of nationalism with political rights, largely failing to abjure imperialism, or affirm the equal legitimacy of different cultures and justified extraterritorial subjugation on the grounds that sovereignty was only legitimate if it was economically dynamic and led to individual autonomy, not social diversity (Mahmud, 1997, 1999; Falk, 2004: 1011; Jaggi, 2000; Parekh, 2008: 45). Colonial conquest was a 'complement' to 'positivist nation-building at home,' with bloodletting legitimized by capitalism and nationalism (Asad, 2005: 2). The linkage between capitalism and nationalism differentiated imperial forms of political organization from prior and alternative styles of governing:

> the rise of democracy *within* the developed world was accompanied by a very contrasted history *without*, the export of liberalism to the less advanced part of the world, be this through colonial rule and its coercive maintenance on the one hand, or the sustaining, in the cold war, of authoritarian regimes on the other.
>
> (Halliday, 2001: 87)

The modern, economic addendum to political citizenship saw the state promise a minimal standard of living. The postmodern, cultural guarantee is access to the technologies of communication. The latter promise derives its force from a sense that political institutions need to relearn what sovereignty is about in polymorphous sovereign states that are diminishingly homogeneous in demographic terms. Heteroglossic populations complicate the executive government's expectation that 'its' people will be faithful to the state while claiming their support as the grounds for its own existence. In Jesús Prieto de Pedro's words:

> The European liberal constitutions of the nineteenth century were political constitutions. . . . The constitutions of the first third of the twentieth century . . . were devoted to economic and social issues . . . another stage is evidenced in the decade of the 1970s in the eruption of cultural concerns: this generates lexical forms and doctrinal categories such as 'cultural rights' . . . the free existence of culture, cultural pluralism, and the access of citizens to culture are guaranteed in intensified forms.
>
> (1999: 63)

This raises complex questions, such as whether minority cultures should be protected from external rule when retention of cultural norms may prevent dynamic change and shackle individual autonomy. For example, should members of a culture be protected by the state from internal oppression when their human rights are compromised in the name of religion, or when the well-being of outsiders is threatened? What should be done about host nations' economic and cultural insecurities, which may be projected onto new arrivals? Should liberalism's lofty but contingent sense of tolerance be celebrated or castigated in contrast to religion's pious intolerance?

Conclusion

Scott's ode to nationalism may resonate with Scotland's struggle and complicity with English empire, but its arrogant denial of identifications beyond the immediate, and fetishization of national unity, is no model for today, tomorrow, or soon. And yet it seems ineradicable. The dilemma that divided dissidents of the postwar Russian empire continues: 'should Sovietization be resisted with cosmopolitanism or nationalism?' (Kristeva, 1997: 8). The cosmic ambivalence of those opening stanzas remains; as Perry Anderson insists, nationalism is 'a mass phenomenon of elemental force in the last two centuries' (1989: 103). And there is a lengthy leftist history of accepting and even promoting the nation 'as the primary mechanism of defense against the domination of foreign and/or global capital' (Hardt and Negri, 2000: 44).

The liberal/UN mantra of demobilization, disarmament, and reintegration as routes to post-conflict peace and prosperity derived from postwar Europe and Japan—taking industrialized fascist countries and reestablishing them after monumental military defeat by state-socialist and state-capitalist ones. The model is barely credible when 'reintegration' means return to a corrupt, hugely unequal, and barely governed nation. The focus on former combatants as problems is understandable, but it misses the reasons for their and others' alienation, and the structural and organizational forces that either incubate or enact violence (Carranza-Franco, 2019). The sovereign state and its attendant ideology is only one of the stresses causing violence.

Notes

1 www.lyricsondemand.com/n/nationalanthemlyrics/usanationalanthemlyrics.html.
2 www.letssingit.com/national-anthems-of-the-world-lyrics-chile-himno-nacional-de-chile-national-anthem-of-chile-76f97f3.
3 https://musicaenmexico.com.mx/himno-nacional-mexicano/.
4 That formulation does allow us to transcend sovereign-state actors and include more complex collectives, albeit ones that seek hegemony over terrain as per states.
5 www.rgs.org/OurWork/Schools/Teaching+resources/Key+Stage+3+resources/The+geography+of+conflict/The+causes+of+conflict.htm; www.hiik.de/en/konfliktbarometer/pdf/ConflictBarometer_2014.pdf.

5 Media

As printed books began to proliferate in the early 18th century, critics feared a return to the 'barbarism' of the post–Roman Empire. Erudition would be overwhelmed by popular texts, just as it had been by war (Chartier, 2004). That raised the prospect of a long-feared 'ochlocracy' of 'the worthless mob' (Pufendorf, 2000: 144) able to share popular texts. In the wake of the French Revolution, Burke was animated by the need to limit popular exuberance via 'restraint upon . . . passions' (1994: 122). And the Industrial Revolution indeed brought new communications technologies, democratic urges, class anxieties, education systems, and knowledges, as well as new forms of imperialism and slavery.

The extension through societies of the capacity to read had as its corollary the possibility of a public that transcended people physically gathered together, with obvious implications: mass literacy could inform industrial and political turmoil. When unionists in the Cuban cigar industry organized readings of news and current affairs to workers on the line, management and the state responded brutally. US slave owners terrorized African Americans who taught themselves and their colleagues to read; Nat Turner's 1831 Rebellion was attributed by many to his literacy. The advent of reading outdoors and the arrival of the train as a new site of public culture generated anxieties about open knowledge and debate. Nineteenth-century US society saw spirited discussions over whether new popular media and genres, such as newspapers, crime stories, and novels, would breed anarchic readers lacking respect for the traditionally literate classes. In other words, the media posed a threat to established elites because they enabled working people to become independently minded and informed, distracting them from servitude (Miller, 1998).

The origins of social psychology can be traced to these anxieties about suddenly urbanized and educated countries. Mill spoke with horror of 'the meanest feelings and most ignorant prejudices of the vulgarest part of the crowd' (1861: 144). Elite theorists emerged from both right and left to explain and deal with these threats, notably Pareto (1976), Mosca (1939), Le Bon (1899), and Michels (1915). They argued that newly literate publics were vulnerable to manipulation by demagogues. James Truslow Adams, Latino founder of the 'American Dream,' saw 'the mob mentality of the city crowd' as 'one of the menaces to modern civilization.' He was especially exercised by 'the prostitution of the moving-picture industry' (1941: 404, 413). These critics were frightened of socialism, democracy, and popular reason (Wallas, 1967: 137). With civil society growing restive, the wealth of radical civic associations was explained away in social-psychological terms rather than political-economic ones.

On the other hand, the media were also welcomed as new forms of life that could bring peace. Communication technology's binding and unbinding of time and space, and the visibility and audibility of signs from elsewhere, stimulated discussion about the possibility of a new world order. The spread of knowledge to all might transcend the chauvinism of sovereign-states (Marvin, 1988: 192–93). Henry Ford announced that 'the airplane and radio know no boundary. They pass over the dotted lines on the map without heed or hindrance. They are binding the world together. . . . Thus may we envision a United States of the World' (1929: 9, 18–19). Marconi said broadcasting could 'make a material contribution towards greater understanding and amity between Nations, the cementing of home life and the happiness of the individual' (1924). Rudolf Arnheim's 1935 'Forecast of Television' predicted the new device would offer viewers simultaneous global experiences, transmitting railway disasters, professorial addresses, town meetings, boxing title fights, dance bands, carnivals, and aerial mountain views—a spectacular *montage* of Broadway and Vesuvius. A common vision could surpass linguistic competence and interpretation. 'The wide world itself enter[ing] . . . our room' via TV might even bring global peace with it, showing spectators that 'we are located as one among many' (1969: 160–63). Two years later, Barrett C. Kiesling suggested the advent of television would 'some day end war' (1937: 248). RCA's David Sarnoff welcomed 'the greatest opportunity ever given us for creating close ties of understanding among the peoples of the world' (2004: 310). Today, Facebook features 'Peace on Facebook' and claims the capacity to 'decrease world conflict' through inter-cultural communication, while Twitter modestly declares itself to be 'a triumph of humanity' ('A Cyber-House,' 2010).

But there remains another side to this happy world of true believers: the world of media effects on audiences and the place of cultural violence. 'The symbolic sphere of our existence—exemplified by religion and ideology, language and art, empirical science and formal science (logic, mathematics)—that can be used to justify or legitimize direct or structural violence' (Galtung, 1990: 291).

The media are crucial components, and war has shaped them irretrievably. The 1914–18 and 1939–45 conflicts left national film production across Europe either shuttered or slowed as conscription led to death, deskilling, and the end of serious competition with Hollywood (Ramsaye, 1947: 7). Those disastrous wars also aided in the development of a raft of media technologies, subsequently handed over to capital (Virilio, 1989). In the contemporary era, so-called smartphones' click wheels, multi-touch screens, global positioning systems, lithium-ion batteries, signal compression, liquid-crystal displays, and various other innovations were the result of funding from the US Defense Advanced Research Projects Agency, the CIA, the US Navy, the US Army Research Office, and the Pentagon (Mazzucato, 2015).

Then there is the role of the media in encouraging or retarding violence among listeners, readers, viewers, and players. This chapter will summarize media effects studies on the subject and then look at the media as sites of violence via their coverage and dramatization of the phenomenon and journalists' own risks. For as military stimuli afforded to the media suggest, the story is much richer than a pure focus on spectatorship can elucidate.

The effect on audiences

Everyone wants to know what role the media play in violence. As soon as US school killings are reported, journalists, police, and scholars rush to see what the perpetrators watched or played on screens. Psychologists assiduously question the relation between playing first-person shooter games and becoming a first-person shooter, while defenders of the representation of violence argue for Aristotle's theories of catharsis, such that high-quality tragic drama can elicit, inform, and purify 'pity and fear' (1995: 988).

Nationwide US media theatrics fail to address the role of religion, race, masculinity, a risk society, or firearms in creating violent people. For instance, following a referral from President Bill Clinton after the 1999 Columbine school shootings, the Federal Trade Commission surveyed studies of 'exposure to violence in entertainment.' After a decade of work, it concluded that consuming violent texts was one factor in youth aggression and violence and generated exaggerated perceptions of the amount of violence (2009). Race? Gender? Gun laws? Protestantism? These were subordinate topics—when they were deemed relevant.

By the early 20th century, academic experts had decreed media audiences to be passive consumers, thanks to the missions of literary criticism (distinguishing the aesthetically cultivated from others) and the psy-function (distinguishing the socially competent from others) (Butsch, 2000: 3). Such tendencies moved into high scholarly gear with the Payne Fund studies of

the 1930s, which juxtaposed the impact of films on 'superior' adults—
'young college professors, graduate students, and their wives'—with children
in juvenile correction centers. That research inaugurated mass social-science
panic about young people at the cinema through the collection of 'authori-
tative and impersonal data which would make possible a more complete
evaluation of motion pictures and their social potentialities' to answer 'what
effect do motion pictures have upon children of different ages?,' especially
on the many young people who were 'retarded' (Charters, 1935: 8, iv–v,
12–13, 31; see Blumer, 1933; Blumer and Hauser, 1933; Dale, 1933; Forman, 1933; May and Shuttleworth, 1933; Mitchell, 1929). Pioneering scholars boldly set out to examine 'The Big Three' narrative themes: love, crime,
and sex. They gauged reactions through autobiographical case studies and
viewers' skin responses, using a psychogalvanometer and beds wired with
hypnographs and polygraphs to record the after-effects of viewing sex and
violence (Charters, 1935: 4, 10, 15, 25, 32, 49, 54, 60; Staiger, 2005: 25;
Wartella, 1996: 173).

The development of the psy-function and communication studies has
led to nine more decades of attempts to correlate youthful consumption
of the popular with violence, emphasizing the size and conduct of audiences to entertainment: where they came from, how many there were,
and what they did as a consequence of being present. Children and the
media remain one of the most politically charged areas of audience study.
Researchers fear Edenic innocents turning into rabid monsters: 'can we
ignore the impact on children of their exposure through television and
films or, more recently, to computer games and arcade video games that
involve vast amounts of violent actions?' (Singer and Singer, 2001: xv).
Worries over the media's indexical power underpin a wealth of research
questioning, testing, and measuring people and texts. Not all this work
assumes a strong relationship between social conduct and audience conduct, but that premise informs it.

Three models dominate the discourse. Social cognitive theory postulates
that screens offer how-to guides for viewers in terms of both means and
motivations for violence. Distribution and cue analysis argues for a more
interactive relationship, such that the media have reciprocal impacts on
social conduct. Arousal theory posits an enabling connection, whereby individuals' tendencies toward violence are heightened by seeing it on screens.
Put together, these paradigms suggest that a number of factors determines
the effects of media violence: its efficacy, its referentiality to actual existence and morality, and the susceptibility of viewers to textual influences in
terms of their individual histories (Comstock, 1989; Comstock and Scharrer, 1999; Cooper, 1996; Surgeon General's Scientific Advisory Committee
on Television and Social Behavior, 1971).

Effects research views the media as forces that can pervert citizens. Entering young minds hypodermically, they can drive people to violence through aggressive and misogynistic images and narratives. This *nostrum* is active at a variety of sites, including laboratories, clinics, prisons, schools, newspapers, psy-function journals, media organizations' research and publicity departments, everyday talk, program-classification regulations, conference papers, congressional debates, advertising agencies, and state-of-our-youth or state-of-our-civil-society moral panics.

Whenever new media technologies emerge, young audiences in particular are immediately identified as both pioneers and victims, simultaneously endowed by manufacturers and critics with immense power and immense vulnerability—early adopters/early naifs. New devices and genres have brought with them marketing techniques focused on the young, even as concerns about supposedly unprecedented and unholy new risks also recur: cheap novels during the 1900s; silent then sound film during the 1920s; radio in the 1930s; comic books of the 1940s and 1950s; pop music and television from the 1950s and 1960s; satanic rock as per the 1970s and 1980s; videocassette recorders in the 1980s; rap music, video games, and the internet since the 1990s; and smartphones, instant messaging systems, and online dating today. Young people are held to be the first to know and the last to understand the media—the grand paradox of youth, latterly on display in the 'digital sublime' of technological determinism, as always with the super-added valence of a future citizenship in peril (Mosco, 2004: 80).

Psy-function research is promoted in the bourgeois media for its claims that children consuming the media are likely to engage in violent conduct (Doughty, 2009). This stimulates public concerns: Argentina's alarmingly named Liga de Amas de Casa, Consumidores y Usuarios (League of Household Warriors, Consumers and Users) conducted a 'Cruzada a favor de la familia y en contra de la TV basura' (Crusade for the Family and Against TV Rubbish), targeting genres that are said to undermine morality, foment violence, glamorize drugs, and distort the minds of the young (Galli, 2005). In Nigeria, critics allege that violent gangs have formed in the 21st century in emulation of US equivalents on TV (Onwumechili, 2007: 138).

Scholars in this tradition generally rely on methodological individualism, failing to account for cultural norms and politics, let alone the arcs of history and waves of geography that situate texts and responses to them inside politics, war, ideology, and discourse. Abundant tests of media effects are based on, as the refrain goes, 'undergraduates at a large university in the Midwest.' When politicians, grant givers, and pundits call for more and more research to prove the media make you violent (or the opposite) the psy-function responds, rarely if ever interrogating its own conditions of existence—namely, that governments, religious groups, and the media themselves use it to account for social problems and engage in the surveillance of popular culture.

This discourse constructs what Harold Garfinkel named the 'cultural dope,' a mythic figure who, in the eyes of these anxious critics, 'produces the stable features of the society by acting in compliance with pre-established and legitimate alternatives of action that the common culture provides.' The 'common sense rationalities . . . of here and now situations' used by people are obscured by this categorization (1992: 68).

Ethnographic research is less cliché. In keeping with the logics of victims' rights, it turns away from those who commit crimes and towards those who suffer from them. For instance, South Asian British women interpreted *The Accused* (dir. Jonathan Kaplan, 1988) as documenting a quite foreign society, with loose controls on misogynistic assault, while Afro-Caribbeans complained about racist associations of people of color with violence in television drama. Class was a lesser source of difference. The most meaningful predictor of position on screen violence was prior exposure to the real thing, which produced concerns about media effects (Schlesinger *et al.*, 1992: 3–4, 164–65).

Such research is supplemented by studies—also at the margins—into how children distinguish between fact and fiction; the generic features and intertexts of children's news, drama, action-adventure, education, cartooning, and play; and how talking about the media encourages social interaction (Buckingham, 2005; Hodge and Tripp, 1986). We can see the benefits here of looking at textual cues, narrative recollection, and emotions among audiences, acknowledging such factors as age, class, gender, and ethnicity. That can help explain why, for example, Australian working-class boys found representations of violence in *Tour of Duty* (1987–90) entertaining. The context was their chance of exposure to actual violence, the futility of their social position, and lack of access to elaborated codes for the purposes of renarrating screen stories (Tulloch and Tulloch, 1993).

As per such work, cultural materialism seeks to erase 'the tenacious division that for so long separated sciences of description and sciences of interpretation, morphological studies and hermeneutical analysis' to recognize that 'the "world of text" . . . [is] a world of objects and performances' (Chartier, 2005a: 38–39). Roger Chartier comprehends the always-contingent meanings of the media in three ways:

- reconstructing 'the diversity of older readings from their sparse and multiple traces';
- focusing on 'the text itself, the object that conveys it, and the act that grasps it'; and

- identifying 'the strategies by which authors and publishers tried to impose an orthodoxy or a prescribed reading on the text.'

(1989: 157, 161–63, 166)

Following in his stead, I seek to track both what happens *in* media texts and what happens *to* them as they travel, attenuating and developing links and discourses across their careers, for it is reductive to understand the media and violence via methods that are purely psy-oriented. The media and their audiences are hybrid monsters, coevally subject to rhetoric, experience, and technology—to text, power, and science—all at once, but in contingent ways (Latour, 1993). Thinking otherwise reduces commodity signs with complex careers to business-as-usual attempts by the US psy-function to blame them for high national levels of interpersonal violence. So let's consider the media as sites of violence through factual and fictional genres and as workplaces.

Journalism

Appalling images of violence have become part of the media's coverage of war, such as the impact of napalm on villagers or military sadism towards prisoners. The meaning of such pictures is not self-evident, for all the visceral emotions they may generate. That meaning is set, fleetingly, by stories, interpretations, and testimony. The claim that such violence is aberrant neglects its simultaneously crucial and banal role in projects of gendered imperial war (Davis, 2003). And the US in particular has a propaganda machine that distorts reality.

Susan D. Moeller's (2004) study of mainstream Yanqui media coverage of state violence between the 1998 nuclear tests in South Asia and the 2003 occupation of Iraq indicates that a wide array of matériel, policies, and practices was essentialized under the emotive sign 'Weapons of Mass Destruction.' It became a 'monolithic menace,' with no distinctions drawn between radiological, nuclear, chemical, or biological weaponry and no recognition that most of these items were made, held, and sold by those countries that were most moralistic about their manufacture, possession, and sale—the United States and Britain.

During that unforgiveable era, media martinet Rupert Murdoch, the ever-Oedipal son of an embedded journalist on the Somme, promised 'We'll do whatever is our patriotic duty,' later intoning that removing التكريتي المجيد عبد حسين صدام (Saddam Hussein Abd al-Majid al-Tikriti) would reduce the price of oil: 'The greatest thing to come out of this for the world economy' (quoted in Solomon, 2001; Greenslade, 2003). Each of the 175 newspapers Murdoch owned across the world endorsed the 2003 invasion (Harvey,

2003: 12). For its part, ABC offered *Profiles from the Front Lines* (2003), an entertainment series produced by Hollywood action-adventure maven Jerry Bruckheimer. It depicted the invasion as you would expect.[1]

In the opening stanza of that assault, half the reports from the thousand US journalists embedded with the invaders depicted combat. None depicted injuries. As the war progressed, the most US residents saw were deeply sanitized images of the wounded from afar, in keeping with 50 contractual terms required of reporters in return for their 'beds.' Even wounded US soldiers were left unnoticed, with no bedside interviews from hospitals. Fallen men and women became the 'disappeared.' News photography commemorated them only via highly misleading, romantic imagery, in stark relief to battleground pictures from World War II and Việt Nam (Miller, 2007). Recall Pat Tillman from Chapter 3.

In the rest of the world's coverage of the Afghan and Iraqi crises, invasions, and occupations, military maneuvers took second place to civilian suffering. Thousands of civilian Afghan deaths reported by South Asian, South-East Asian, Western European, and Arabic news services went essentially unnoticed in the US, because they could not be 'verified' by journalists/officials (Miller, 2007).

Away from such complicity with Pentagon propaganda, many of the world's reporters

> venture into the darkest corners to shed light on current events. A considerable number of them are subjected to intimidation, physical violence, kidnapping or illegal detention in direct relation to their work and, in extreme cases, they can be killed because of their professional activity.
> (United Nations Office on Drugs and Crime, 2014)

The 'killing of a journalist is a sign of deteriorating respect for human rights,' and frequently produces repressive reactions from the state that only further the rate and number of violent political crimes (Gohdes and Carey, 2017).

The Committee to Protect Journalists estimates that 1,842 reporters have been killed worldwide since 1992.[2] Although the deaths of war correspondents are often heavily reported as headline stories, local investigative reporters are more vulnerable: 93% of journalists murdered between 2002 and 2013 were working in their own countries, often executed by criminal gangs threatened by media exposure (González de Bustamante and Relly, 2016; Gohdes and Carey, 2017; International Federation of Journalists, 2019). The Council of Europe rates press freedom across Europe 'more fragile than at any time since the end of the Cold War' because of violence and obstructiveness. Death threats doubled in 2018 on the previous year, as did impunity (2019: 5, 8, 16). Such violence occurs both in overtly conflicted countries and putatively peaceful ones (von der Lippe and Ottosen, 2016; Löfgren Nilsson and Örnebring, 2016; Jungblut and Hoxha, 2016).

Chema Suárez Serrano's meta-analysis concludes that 'aggression against those who tell the truth does not discriminate between times of peace and war, professional journalists or citizens, not even the channel through which they send their messages' (2016: 27). Hun Shik Kim notes that in Latin America, 'political upheaval and turmoil not only force journalists to confront legal restrictions and political persecution, but also put the journalists at risk of physical intimidation and targeted killings' (2010: 485). Interviews across the region confirm the fact (Saldaña and Mourão, 2018). Perhaps 500 Latin American reporters disappeared or were assassinated between 2000 and mid-2017 (Díaz Nosty and de Frutos García, 2017).

Assaults on journalistic integrity are not only physical, thanks to online platforms (Löfgren Nilsson and Örnebring, 2016; Yardi and Boyd, 2010). Prevalent forms of harassment have expanded from physical attacks to swearing, defamation, calumny, trolling, stalking, and threats of sexual assault and murder. Pressures come not only from systematically violent groups or parties to particular disputes, but everyday citizens who dislike what they read (Cook and Heilmann, 2013). Such aggression stimulates cultural and emotional differences; some reporters react to threats with greater resilience (or foolhardiness) than others (Høiby and Ottosen, 2015).

Across the globe, the frequently gendered nature of threats is clear (Ferrier, 2019). The experience of reporting war, as opposed to commenting on it, is very gendered. While women journalists sometimes get entrée denied to men in terms of human-interest stories, personal confessions, and family perspectives, they are routinely excluded and patronized by everyone from translators to editors-in-chief—told that the front is no place for a woman. We need all war correspondents, women and men alike, to be alert to gendered questions as a core component of their work, as per the examples of Maggie O'Kane in Bosnia or Jamie Tarabay and Sabrina Tavernise in Iraq.

Moving away from war, let's examine an individual narrative: the role of the media in the 1993 murder in Britain's Liverpool of two-year-old James Bulger by preteens Robert Thompson and Jon Venables and its aftermath, which continues today. Video was said to have:

- caused the crime (one of the killers grew up in a household with 64 violent and/or pornographic tapes);
- illustrated the boys' callousness (they looked at cartoons after the death); and
- ensured their conviction (it captured them in the shopping mall and they were interrogated before it in custody)

So the screen was held responsible for desire to murder, absence of contrition, and proof of guilt. The abduction was captured by a shopping-mall security camera. Then the search was on to explain why Thompson and Venables killed the little boy. Venables's father had just rented *Child's Play 3* (dir. Jack Bender, 1991). It was analyzed for tropes in the Bulger case (train tracks, paint splattering, battery use, and child abduction; much was also made of a woman's report that her six-year-old son had 'become possessed' after seeing it, the evidence being his attempt to kill the family pet). The two boys were problematized because they watched cartoons after the killing and interrogated on video over 12 hours, replayed in court. These recordings showed police encouraging Venables to narrate the events in filmic terms. He did so through a fictional story that was then judged to be an historical account and hence a confession (Miller, 1998).

But that was not the end to the media's role in this event. A decade later, video game developer Legacy Interactive promoted *Law and Order II* with a picture of James Bulger from closed-circuit TV in the mall, to enduring controversy (Boyer, 2007). In 2009, Australian's Channel Seven used his death to market *City Homicide* (2007–11) (Reilly, 2009). Twenty-five years after the crime, Venables was convicted—for a second time—of having child pornography on a computer ('James Bulger Killer,' 2018). And when a short film reconstructing the murder, *Detainment* (dir. Vincent Lambe, 2018) was nominated for an Academy Award as Best Live Action Short—a film made against the wishes of the murdered child's family—there was outrage (Hammad, 2019).

For a quarter of a century, the media had been crucial to the killing and its aftermath: as causal agent, sign of criminality, proof of guilt, marketing, evidence of commercial and artistic corruption, and site of complaint for the family. The media's relation to violence is not only about their effect on people as incentives, as this capsule history indicates.

Fiction

Consider crime fiction. The genre constructs a viewing position that accepts the state monopoly on the exercise of 'legitimate' violence in the protection of private property, private morality, and human safety. Whereas 1950s and 1960s TV police drama concentrated on social landscapes and professional life, programs since then have tended to construct interiority for their characters. Emotional tendencies merge with action sequences and office work to produce soap-operatic forms, brokering the relationship between the private and public spheres (Tulloch, 1990: 69–70, 72). Notable recent instances include *Dexter* (2006–13), *Ófærð* (*Trapped*) (2015–present), *Marcella* (2016–present), and *Unité 42* (*Unit 42*) (2017–present). Personal and professional lives intertwine inexorably, creepily, and multi-generationally.

Ernest Mandel tied the success of crime novels, in all their gory detail, to the split subjectivity produced by mass-consumption capitalism (1984: 61–62, 65): mounting mechanization, diverse commodity production, hyper-consumerism, and increasingly alienated populations. He argued that the search for identity was a necessary process for fiction produced in such societies. People were divided among a variety of selves: workers, buyers, and capitalists. As proprietors of homes and consumables, they upheld and even materialized laws of ownership, of both objects and people. But as citizens, they were concerned with the general good rather than their own. And as sexual subjects, they were driven by needs that took them beyond reason, the family, and property.

Such stories enact the dilemmas posed by this contradictory subjectivity. They reference law and order, the where and why of sovereignty, in a physical, material way, via the daily actions of agents acting as delegates of a people, monarchy, or military. The arbitrariness of this delegation, and its reliance on instant decision and action, is paradoxical. Loading up officials with power and responsibility, and hence signing away the right to democracy, makes the myth of bourgeois society—popular endorsement of overt governmental processes through the publicly ratified rule of law—unsustainable (Mandel, 1984: 65, 122).

Violence is also central to telenovelas. The genre derives most immediately from soap operas, but its genealogy originates with the melodrama, which was critically damned from its beginnings in 18th-century Europe because of a high-tensile emotionalism that contrasted with latter-day naturalism and realism. The melodrama can also be read as a site for trying out new identities at a time of intense social disruption, when religious and monarchical power was being challenged by urbanizing capitalism and secular democracy (Merritt, 1983). The genre's revolutionary referent recurred in the 1940s and 1950s with the re-establishment of gender normativity after the war; Hollywood's melodramas and films noirs featured hysterical men unsettled by both time away and their return (Cunningham, 1981). This references Aristotle's distinction between history and drama, favoring the latter because of its capacity for the general and the complex, the explanatorily powerful and conflictual (1961: 68, 111).

Today's pro-capitalist violence of the narcotics trade in the Americas has been frequently and lucratively dramatized on TV via *narconovelas*, notably from Colombia, Brazil, México, and Venezuela, and recently made for gullible Anglo eyes, ears, and nostrils. The Netflix series *Narcos* (2015–present) is as guilty of historical inaccuracy as it is insistent on having diligently recorded reality. The company says over 60 million people have devoured its ode to rivers of blood (Britto, 2016; Marcos, 2018).

Gabriel García Márquez viewed the success of narco genres, in both literature and television, as indicative of an ongoing popular fascination with the abject, the cruel, and the spectacular, embodied in a male rule-breaking that no amount of positive stereotypes could wish away: the *narconovela* takes the seemingly inevitable, inexorable violence that characterizes Latin American history and fixes the population between desire and futility, passion and resignation, celebration and denial (Vásquez, 2013). It's significant that many men publicly defend it as embodying popular values: support for the church, family, loyalty, and friendship. They argue that narco excess and violence are products of a society that excludes them and people like them—many of the people watching—from power, comfort, and pleasure (Rincón, 2015).

Narconovelas cover sex, violence, and upward mobility (de Pablos, 2019). They succeed in international markets thanks to a blend of the traditional emotional intensity of melodrama with the violence and high production values of action adventure, providing broadcast television with an answer to its newer audiovisual competitors and attracting key audiences for advertisers (Piñon, 2019). The genre offers a cosmically ambivalent transformation of this limiting story—a site where women may pursue power, autonomy, riches, and pleasure through sex and clientelism, but in ways that draw a textual and social condemnation and harks back to the still-present past via *Marianismo* and *machismo*'s contradictory placements within tradition and modernity, continuity and transcendence, family and singularity (Ramírez Murcia, 2016).

Narcotrafficking and its core violence are glamorized in ways that play up both a rejection of traditional political-economic institutions and a reassertion of traditional identities. Narcos and their apparatchiks embody upward mobility in societies where the prospect of uplift via education and industriousness is minimal because life chances are dominated by birth and race; hence popular reason embracing *narcotraficantes*' (narcotraffickers) spectacular bling (Rincón, 2015).

Narconovelas offer a cocktail of violence. Women are often abused and humiliated. Male sexual desire, illicit money, unwarranted assault, and cavalier killing are glamorized. The state is absent or corrupt. This fetish of capital brings together the extraordinary violence of primary accumulation with the secondary accumulation of advanced capitalism (Rincón, 2018; Martín-Barbero, 2004). In 2014, the Venezuelan and Panamanian establishments (*Chavistas* in Caracas and the right in Panama City) sought to ban *narconovelas* for glorifying cruelty and drugs; left and right were equally appalled (Rincón, 2015; Caselli, 2016).

For some affected in real life by the violence these programs depict, it is not so easy to embrace the genre and its use of *Marianismo*. Yet certain series criticize the violent misogyny they portray, even as they offer audiences the risky pleasures of narco luxury and taboo-breaking (Cabañas, 2012).

And fiction arguably documents such violence more effectively than news and current affairs (Rincón, 2019). It has the potential to question inequality and display, much as Warner Bros.' gangster films did for the United States in the 1930s. One moment responds to the mass unemployment of the Depression and the prohibition of alcohol by heroizing gangsters; the other reacts to the destabilization of globalization and the prohibition of cocaine by heroizing gangsters (Sklar, 1992; Giraldo, 2015).

Conclusion

As per the introduction's anecdote about the filming of *24* that wasn't, lines between fact and fiction blur in US war coverage, the James Bulger killing, and the *novela*. Consider the polyvalence of VH1's reality TV show *Cartel Crew* (2019–present), which features close relatives of dead or imprisoned narcos. These offspring may themselves have been in the joint, or benefited directly or indirectly from their parents' illegal wealth; but now, they are putatively on the straight. Michael Corleone (yes) Blanco is prominent, because his mom, Griselda Blanco de Trujillo, killed over 200 people during her reign of terror (Nolasco, 2019). She was portrayed on screen by Catherine Zeta-Jones in *Cocaine Godmother* (2018).[3] Blanco says

> I'm all for J. Lo playing my mother. She was one of my original choices. Catherine Zeta-Jones' project was great as well. I'm all for it. Anything that I can lend consultation on my life. As long as it's a lucrative project. . . . As long as the story is told correctly from the horse's mouth.
>
> (quoted in Nolasco, 2019)

Cartel Crew is pretty standard fare, in two ways: it is part of Hollywood's 90-years-and-counting glorification of mafia killers and involves the predictable contretemps and resolutions between participants of reality programs, plus deep and meaningless exchanges between pseudo-best-friends-forever (Carras, 2019).

The second season featured Emma Coronel Aispuro. Her husband is Joaquín Archivaldo Guzmán Loera, better known as 'El Chapo' (The Little Guy). She was represented in *El Chapo*, a 2019 miniseries. In the words of Senator John N. Kennedy's protest against *Cartel Crew*:

> Since establishing his crime syndicate in the late 1980s, El Chapo has been responsible for the deaths of hundreds of thousands of people, both through direct violence and the devastating impact of drug addiction. At one point in time, El Chapo was on the Federal Bureau of

Investigation's World's Most Wanted Fugitives List, second only to Osama bin Laden.

(2019)

The justification for Coronel's appearance is that she wants to share her pain (stigmatization) with fellow-sufferers and follow Michael Corleone Blanco's model: he sells clothing, cell phone covers, and coffee cups branded with his mom ('We have businesses, like every other American. . . . We're trying to live the American dream, you know?,' quoted in Nolasco, 2019). The line is called 'Pure Blanco.' He is diversifying into cannabis. Coronel wants to emulate Blanco's success with fashion and other items named after her husband.

And the verdict on Coronel's debut? Murdoch's *New York Post* deemed it 'classy' (Vincent, 2019). The *Washington Post* noted, more soberly, that her husband had signed off on the use of his name to sell smartphone cases, frocks, and hats (Armus, 2019). Mexican journalists reacted with horror at any glorification, or even humanization, of such people, be they money launderers or courtiers of the horror that engulfs the country (Nájar, 2019).[4] In Ioan Grillo's words, it was

a sick and terrible decision by VH1 to have El Chapo's wife Emma Coronel on its reality show 'Cartel Crew.' There is a humanitarian catastrophe in Mexico from cartel violence. This is not a glamorous reality show. Where are images of mass graves?[5]

But little if anything was said about the US network Telemundo broadcasting a half-hour interview in 2018 dedicated to humanizing her and her husband.[6] And Coronel? In the episode in question, she avows that despite the hardships she has suffered—and continues to experience—she will 'stay positive' ('Así fue,' 2019).

Violence and its textualization are irrevocably interlaced. Just as it is impossible to come up with a singular definition of violence and have it implemented universally in legal or statistical forms, so the taste for incarnating violence on stage, page, and screen is insatiable. That taste is matched by efforts to hold the media accountable for violence, thereby eluding uncomfortable questions about social relations: gender, religion, nation, and so on. While we all need to be familiar with media-centric debates about effects on audiences' violent conduct, more productive discussions can ensue from seeing the meeting-point of violence and the media in terms of inadequate reporting due to nationalistic bigotry, the perils of journalists, the unworthy glamorization of gangsters, and the complexities of drawing clear distinctions between fact and fiction.

Notes

1 www.youtube.com/watch?v=4bsZJOcUCx0.
2 https://cpj.org/data/killed/?status=Killed&type%5B%5D=Journalist&start_year= 1992&end_year=2018&group_by=year.
3 www.youtube.com/watch?v=cIefEWw2Fng.
4 www.youtube.com/watch?v=vcsK8JhRuV0.
5 https://twitter.com/ioangrillo.
6 www.youtube.com/watch?v=N0tMZBT2ykw.

Conclusion

With Richard Maxwell

Discourses about violence are in a constant duel over individual and collective psychology, religiosity, ideology, masculinity, nationalism, legitimacy, and meaning. This has been a book about the circulation of those discourses and their switching points/intersections.

Fifty years ago, Hannah Arendt argued that violence was the 20th century's 'common denominator.' This was due to the threat of absolute destruction posed by nuclear weaponry (1970: 3)—an extension of Eisenhower's argument about the military-industrial complex referred to earlier.

Thirty years ago, we awaited a peace dividend. The Cold War had ended, so much of the world's expenditure on violence could be redirected towards social services and the Global South and away from the military-industrial complex (Ward and Davis, 1992; Knight *et al.*, 1996). It didn't happen. The amount that wealthy countries spend on the military shows how right Eisenhower was and how deleterious that has been for their economies and societies (Desli and Gkoulgkoutsika, 2020).

So do we live in a more or less violent world than before; and if it has changed, how and why? Are movements such as #MeToo and Black Lives Matter signs of new turns in acknowledging violence and preventing it? And what will be the ongoing impact of Covid-19?

Writing towards the close of the Second World War, Orwell saw the return of utopias he had encountered just prior to the First:

> Reading recently a batch of rather shallowly optimistic 'progressive' books, I was struck by the automatic way in which people go on repeating certain phrases which were fashionable before 1914. Two great favourites are 'the abolition of distance' and 'the disappearance of frontiers.' I do not know how often I have met with the statements that 'the aeroplane and the radio have abolished distance' and 'all parts of the world are now interdependent.'
>
> (1944)

We remain consumed by dualities that have shadowed much of this volume—between a *dys*topia of essentially selfish, wicked, desperate people who must be held in check by the state and a *u*topia of fundamentally thoughtful, good, charitable folk who form civil society.

At the time of writing, much of the world is convulsed by a pandemic. It is unusual in the last century, because it has initially wrought more devastation in the Global North than the Global South. Typical antinomies are in play. On one side is a predicted return to a supposedly transcended latent savagery lurking within us all, initially indexed in overly vigorous supermarket contests for sanitary masks, toilet paper, and packaged food. Survivalists await the second coming of the *Lord of the Flies* (Golding, 1954), with guns, ammunition, and ideology at the ready in well-stocked shelters (AFP and Borbon, 2020; Diss, 2020). When US politicians attempt to censor scientists fighting both the climate crisis and this virus, many of us picture billionaires equipping their bunkers with materials 'liberated' from public storage (Rupar, 2020; Waters, 2018; Johnson, 2020).

On the other side lies a Panglossian celebration, a supposed renewal of civil society (Rusbridger, 2020). This is allegedly evident from Mediterranean and Manhattan terrace- and stoop-dwellers serenading health professionals and their derring-do, citizens collecting food for those in need, and folks finding innovative ways to make love not war, teach their children well, and take exercise. It's the putative equivalent of 1940s liberators or the spirit of the Blitz—in fact an horrendous moment of British murder, sexual assault, and non-violent criminality (Overy, 2020); but not to worry, chaps.

Reports proliferate of abusive men luxuriating in the additional power over their female partners provided by lockdowns, insisting they not leave the house for fear of infection, or murdering them (Gearin and Knight, 2020; Parkinson, 2020). We hear of general surges in the crime rate ('Coronavirus,' 2020). Colombia closed its borders completely, even to citizens seeking return. That Draconian prohibition did nothing to curb the terrible wave of violence against indigenous environmental defenders, who are slaughtered week after week by right-wing criminals working for shady, shadowy mining corporations (Oquendo, 2020). Meanwhile, Mexican authorities monitored sizeable social-media groups dedicated to sacking supermarkets and inciting others to do the same (Camhaji, 2020).

We remain haunted by the scarred and scarring nature of violence, the strange, ongoing dialectic of states that are either too present or too absent—able to coerce/unable to serve—and prevailing religious and sexual dogmas.

Novelists, essayists, activists, survivors, fighters, and social scientists have all endeavored to explain the long and disturbing history of violence

(Farnsworth-Alvear *et al.*, 2017). These *violentólogos* list numerous causes (García Villegas, 2015):

- machismo
- systematic class inequality
- racial discrimination
- Marxism
- the United States, China, Russia, France, and the UK
- the Janus face of neoliberalism, as a blend of economic deregulation and statist reformation of citizens
- cross-generational oligarchies
- economic inequality
- paramilitaries and organized crime
- drug dealing and the criminal economy in general
- states riddled with corruption; and
- public distrust of the police, judiciary, and politics

Violence is so multifaceted, so deeply embedded in culture and statecraft, so much a part of ideology and gender relations, so tightly tethered to colonial history, that it is inescapable. For example, the bloodshed in Latin America is stupefying, as the figures you've read indicate (Grillo, 2016). Why is there so much sexual torture, much of it of men by men? Why are people unconnected to the drug trade selected for mass slaughter by its agents? Where do torturers and assassins begin and the military and police end their jurisdictions, identities, and actions? Where does evangelical Christianity's weird cultism fit in?

In violent countries, the state is laden with violence and corruption. In violent homes, men are driven by anger, frustration, and entitlement against others in their lives, notably women. In wartime, the military is compelled by a logic of obedience in the name of instrumental reason. On the sports field, athletes operate through an admixture of personal glory and collective expression of power.

A profound cynicism about politics and government animates violence. It relates to the oligopolies and oligarchies of everyday life, colonial hangovers, and the incomplete project of citizenship. Profoundly unequal societies in terms of wealth, education, and health see organized criminality peak. Tipping points are reached, but not necessarily with real success, as Mexican marches against mass murder have shown—sudden expressions of civil society that bring hope and romance, then slide back into a collective hopelessness.

Commodities are all too often crucial elements in these struggles. It is easy and right to castigate the Global North as a supplier of arms (which it thinks should be legal) and a consumer of drugs (which it thinks should not). But consider also the book you are reading. It was written with the aid of gold for circuitry, tin for solder, tungsten for capacitors, and tantalum. These 'conflict minerals' form part of our electronic devices. Most come from the Democratic Republic of Congo. They have funded the country's ongoing civil war, in which millions of lives have been lost. Militias control mines through murder, sexual abuse, and rape. They work alongside dozens of Chinese and Indian companies, merrily profiting from a workforce laden with thousands of pre-teen children that provides materials to manufacturers who subcontract with the companies you know and love, from Apple to Samsung. For many involved, it is notoriously difficult to ascertain the origins of these metals once processed ore is mixed with the overall global supply, then sold on the international market ('Progress and Challenges of Conflict Minerals,' 2018; United States Government Accountability Office, 2018; Kara, 2018; Scheele *et al.*, 2016; Laudati and Mertens, 2019; Callaway, 2017).

Just as self-indulgent Global Northerners need to stop whining about their cocaine addictions and start thinking about the commodity trail that brings them their pitiful pleasures, so we should study that same trail that brings us our tools of work and play.

Resources of hope

The tendency towards violence is never far from the surface, but nor are alternatives. For alongside the horrors of both everyday life and the spectacular, we must consider equally human tendencies: pacific and welcoming daily conduct, vibrant social movements, dogged newsgathering, astringent cultural critique, and innovative scientific endeavor. They are just as persistent as the violence they oppose. And it is possible to see world history not only as a succession of waves of horror punctuated by perilous peace, but as a series of settlements that expand the definition and exercise of citizenship. Together they comprise resources of hope.

And think of the positive side to sports. Brecht joyously said: 'We have our eye on those huge concrete pans, filled with 15,000 men and women of every variety of class and physiognomy, the fairest and shrewdest audience in the world' (1964: 6–8). He saw great potential for political vibrancy and even revolution, akin to the pleasure that John Lennon experienced when football crowds chanted the Beatles' song 'All Together Now' to express solidarity (1971). Lukács held that proletarian crowds truly understood the importance of football, because it was an extension in spectacular form of their industrial experience (1972). América Larraín overcame her intense antipathy to the sport because it encapsulating identity through movement

(2015). Jean Rouch's cinema illustrated the ties between dance and football (2003). Bonaventura de Sousa Santos argues that popular resistance to the Brazilian dictatorship that led to progressive local government was fomented by the formation of clubs, inter alia (2007: 311–12), while Cabral took football teams as models for the unity of purpose and diversity of identity needed for revolutionary change (1979: 4).

There are interesting contradictions between militant nationalistic men cavorting in stadia against 'the other,' given that the symbols that engulf them and they choose are often so international. The sport itself embodies global culture as much as do the English or Spanish languages (Hobsbawm, 1998: 6). Ulrich Beck avowed that football counters nationalism thanks to its postcolonial/global capitalist ecumenism, and it can work for multicultural peacefulness—the positive side of multinational capital striding the stadia of the world (2002). Jacques Attali deems it one of the few topics that can generate discussion in almost any venue, potentially leading to a common understanding where none had seemed possible (2001: 262). Néstor Garcia Canclini notes that teams are 'key sites of imaginary identity,' capable of producing 'a durable, affective investment of loyalty and solidarity' (2008: 393). Even Orwell referred admiringly to a miner who emerged from the pit covered from head to toe by coal dust, then proudly washed and changed into his best clothes to attend a match, imagining a socialist future that would sparkle with the pleasure of watching football (1958: 3, 11).

Sports embody domination, scientific management, and an artificially generated dislike of others, but also collaboration, spontaneity, and fellowship. Against their banal competitiveness and disciplinary obsessions stands the untrammeled ecstasy of catching a wave—a perfectly material, utopian, snatched alternative to this seemingly most capitalistic of metaphors. Hence the paradox at the heart of sports, its simultaneously transcendent and imprisoning qualities and astonishing capacity to allegorize.

The developing discourse of human rights as cosmopolitan citizenship is another hopeful sign, especially as it expands to take account of health, education, and money. The discourse was trumpeted after the Second World War as the West's mea culpa for fascism and source of ethical superiority over Marxism-Leninism and Maoism. It has only been contingent in its condemnation of violence, and in many 'a clash between the audiography of voiced human rights concerns and the map of geopolitical interests . . . the latter mutes voices and compromises justice' (Shapiro, 2015: 26). But the claptrap about national values versus human rights needs to end, given the anti-queer, anti-feminist policies of theocracies; the racial formations underpinning authoritarianism; the horror of war, torture, and capital punishment; and so on (Hunter, 2009; Worden, 2008).

Let's return to Covid-19. Despite the cynicism expressed earlier, something is happening.

People in quarantine celebrate their nurses and doctors, hospital staff, and other frontline workers every evening with noisy appreciation. They know who matters, and they bang their pots to make the point. Grocery workers are essential; hospital janitors are essential; teachers are essential. Wall Street and fossil-fuel capital have no value in this humanitarian crisis, no meaning now. Clear skies treat *Chilang@s* (residents of Mexico City) to fresh air. Londoners and New Yorkers aren't subjected to soot on their windowsills and lank, disgusting hair. The sweet sounds of birds singing are no longer interrupted by honking horns. Seismic activity around the planet has diminished. While people pause their pursuit of unnecessary consumption, tourism, and waste, waterways are cleansing themselves (Koren, 2020). Why would we want moguls and militarists to return to their destructive ways in a post-pandemic world? They are not role models of honesty and trustworthiness in the realm of ecosystems and human health.

The dystopic and utopic aspects of the crisis align with two curves—the rising apex versus the flattening graph. We can call their imaginary adherents the fat-curvers versus the flat-curvers. Fat-curvers are typically anti-science promoters of business as usual: they do little to nothing to stop the spike in infections and deaths, brought to us by neoliberal just-in-time healthcare, and abdicate responsibility for their role in the disaster. The reason so many folks have accepted and even favored economic and social policies against their own self-interest has been their conjoined love of money and loathing of expertise—the sense that those who speak out against educational and policy elites do so with a common touch that promises upward mobility (Chua, 2018).

One side effect of the viral crisis has been that the mad and maddening idiocy of much folk knowledge—such as Mexican President López Obrador[1] showing off his amulet that allegedly protects him from Covid-19 and telling us that if we give ourselves over to Jesus Christ we shall all be saved from it—is sometimes slowly, sometimes quickly, being exposed and countered. The populist denunciation of expertise by charlatans around the globe is looking as hollow as it was once effective. But it illustrates what is truly an incomplete project of citizenship:

> we all too easily take a non-sectarian civil life for granted, forgetting that in a proselytising religious culture it stands as an exceptional accomplishment. In fact the separation of spiritual discipline from secular government and conscience from law was never complete. It remains our own unfinished business, a contest unresolved since early modern times.
> (Saunders, 1997: viii)

Today, scientists are being singled out as heroes (Stevis-Grindneff, 2020). They have shown what global cooperation can achieve when oleaginous profiteers, god-bothering charlatans, and military blandishments are sidelined.

Flat-curvers are not just creators of statistical projections that suggest eventually diminished rates of infection (Allain, 2020). They demand a break with the past in order to provide and receive that all-important obligation of care—a collective duty to act in the service of all. If we self-isolate and stay well, we free up a hospital bed for someone in need. If we flatten the curve, our use of vital materials declines and we can pass spare supplies on to the next population in need of care. China helps New York, which helps Detroit, New Orleans, or Chicago. Cuba and China aid France, Italy, Spain, Venezuela, and Iran; they in turn assist others (Countercurrents Collective, 2020). Flat curving is an anti-viral social contract.

That renewed solidarity, however compromised by religion, gender, beliefs, borders, financial interest, media bloviation, or anything else, is crucial in the attempt to diminish violence, both collectively and inter-personally.

If we can find ways of persuading the public that expenditure on the overseas repressive state apparatus is wasteful, that academic knowledge can be valuable, that religion is obsessed with power and control, and that hegemonic masculinity has been bad for the vast majority of people, then violence can indeed be reduced.

Note

1 www.youtube.com/watch?v=Hf6vI5uODYc.

Works cited

Abrahamian, Ervand. (2003). "The US Media, Huntington and September 11." *Third World Quarterly* 24, no. 3: 529–44.

Ackerly, Brooke A., Maria Stern, and Jacqui True, eds. (2006). *Feminist Methodologies for International Relations*. Cambridge: Cambridge University Press.

Adams, Alex. (2017). "'The Sweet Tang of Rape': Torture, Survival and Masculinity in Ian Fleming's Bond Novels." *Feminist Theory* 18, no. 2: 137–58.

Adams, James Truslow. (1941). *The Epic of America*. New York: Triangle Books.

Adorno, Theodor W. (1945). "A Social Critique of Radio Music." *Kenyon Review* 7, no. 2: 208–17.

Adorno, Theodor W. (1997). "Opinion Delusion Society." Trans. Henry W. Pickford. *Yale Journal of Criticism* 10, no. 2: 227–45.

Adorno, Theodor W. (2005). *Critical Models: Interventions and Catchwords*. Trans. Henry W. Pickford. New York: Columbia University Press.

Adorno, Theodor W. (2007). *Negative Dialectics*. Trans. E. B. Ashton. New York: Continuum.

Adorno, Theodor W. (2010). "Education After Auschwitz." *Canadian International Youth Letter*, http://paep.ca/doc/CIYL%20-%20Theodor%20Adorno%20-%20 Education%20after%20Auschwitz.pdf.

Adorno, Theodor W., Else Frenkel-Brunswick, Daniel J. Levinson, and R. Nevitt Sanford. (1950). *The Authoritarian Personality*. New York: Harper & Row.

Adorno, Theodor W. and Max Horkheimer. (1979). *Dialectic of the Enlightenment*. Trans. John Cumming. London: Verso.

AFP and Christian Borbon. (2020, March 17). "Coronavirus Panic Buying: The Psychology Behind Toilet Paper Hoarding." *Gulf News*, https://gulfnews.com/ photos/news/coronavirus-panic-buying-the-psychology-behind-toilet-paper-hoarding-1.1584423699719?slide=1.

Agnew, Robert and David M. Petersen. (1989). "Leisure and Delinquency." *Social Problems* 36, no. 4: 332–50.

Agustín, Laura Maria. (2007). *Sex at the Margins: Migration, Labour Markets and the Rescue Industry*. London: Zed Books.

Ahluwalia, Pal, Louise Bethlehem, and Ruth Ginio. (2007). "Introduction: 'Unsettling Violence'." *Violence and Non-Violence in Africa*. Ed. Pal Ahluwalia, Louise Bethlehem, and Ruth Ginio. London: Routledge. 1–11.

"Alarma y repudio en Colombia por ataques con ácido." (2014, April 4). *BBC Mundo*, www.bbc.com/mundo/noticias/2014/04/140404_colombia_ataques_acido_wbm.

Allain, Rhett. (2020, March 24). "The Promising Math Behind 'Flattening the Curve'." *Wired*, www.wired.com/story/the-promising-math-behind-flattening-the-curve/.

Allende, Salvador. (2018). *Discursos de Salvador Allende*. N. p.: Biblioteca Clodomiro Almeyda/Partido Socialista de Chile.

Alliez, Éric and Antonio Negri. (2003). "Peace and War." *Theory, Culture & Society* 20, no. 2: 109–18.

Althusser, Louis. (1969). *For Marx*. Trans. Ben Brewster. Harmondsworth: Penguin.

Althusser, Louis. (1977). *Lenin and Philosophy and Other Essays*. Trans. Ben Brewster. London: New Left Books.

Altman, Daniel. (2015). "The Strategist's Curse: A Theory of False Optimism as a Cause of War." *Security Studies* 24, no. 2: 284–315.

"America Is the Only Rich Country That Has Frequent Mass Shootings." (2019, August 8). *Economist*, www.economist.com/leaders/2019/08/08/america-is-the-only-rich-country-that-has-frequent-mass-shootings.

"America's Gun Culture in Charts." (2019, August 5). *BBC News*, www.bbc.com/news/world-us-canada-41488081.

Amin, Samir. (1997). *Capitalism in the Age of Globalization*. London: Zed Books.

Amnesty International. (2018). *Death Sentences and Executions 2017*, www.amnesty.org.au/wp-content/uploads/2018/04/amnesty-report-death-penalty-2018.pdf.

Anderson, Perry. (1989). *Considerations on Western Marxism*. London: Verso.

Andrews, David L. (2006). "Introduction: Playing with the Pleasure Principle." *South Atlantic Quarterly* 105, no. 2: 269–76.

"A New Approach is Needed to Tackle Violent Crime in London." (2018, October 24). Economist, https://www.economist.com/graphic-detail/2018/10/24/a-new-approach-is-needed-to-tackle-violent-crime-in-london.

Anolik, Lili. (2018, June 28). "Lorena Bobbitt's American Dream." *Vanity Fair*, www.vanityfair.com/style/2018/06/lorena-bobbitt-john-wayne-bobbitt-25-years.

Arango Arias, Ana Lucía and Carlos Andrés Hurtado Díaz. (2012). "Especificaciones sobre la explotación sexual comercial de niños, niñas y adolescentes (ESCNNA), el turismo sexual y sus relaciones con el discurso capitalista." *Textos y Sentidos* 6: 79–101.

Arendt, Hannah. (1970). *On Violence*. San Diego: Harcourt Brace Jovanovich.

Aristotle. (1961). *Poetics*. Trans. S. H. Butcher. New York: Hill and Wang.

Aristotle. (1963). "Politics." Trans. Benjamin Jowett. *Social and Political Philosophy: Readings from Plato to Gandhi*. Ed. John Somerville and Ronald E. Santoni. New York: Doubleday. 59–100.

Aristotle. (1995). *The Complete Works of Aristotle: The Revised Oxford Translation*. Vol. 1 and 2. Ed. Jonathan Barnes. Princeton: Princeton University Press.

Armstrong, Gary. (1998). *Football Hooligans: Knowing the Score*. Oxford: Berg.

Armus, Teo. (2019, November 19). "'Sick and Terrible': VH1 Reality Show Slammed for Featuring El Chapo's Wife." *Washington Post*, www.washingtonpost.com/nation/2019/11/19/reality-show-slammed-el-chapo-wife/?outputType=amp.

Arnheim, Rudolf. (1969). *Film as Art*. London: Faber and Faber.

Arnold, Matthew. (2003). *Culture and Anarchy*. Project Gutenberg, www.gutenberg.org/dirs/etext03/7cltn10.txt.

Asad, Talal. (2005). "Reflections on Laïcité & the Public Sphere." *Items and Issues* 5, no. 3: 1–11.

"Así fue el debut de Emma Coronel, pareja de 'El Chapo', en el Cartel Crew." (2019, November 11). *Milenio*, www.milenio.com/espectaculos/famosos/emma-coronel-esposa-chapo-debut-cartel-crew.

Attali, Jacques. (2001). *Bruits: Essais sur l'économie politique de la musique*, 2nd ed. Paris: Librairie Arthème Fayard/Presses Universitaires de France.

Augustine. (1998). *Confessions*. Trans. Henry Chadwick. Oxford: Oxford University Press.

Australian Domestic and Family Violence Death Review Network. (2018). *Data Report 2018*, https://lst.org.au/wp-content/uploads/2018/07/ADFVDRN_Data_Report_2018_.pdf.

Australian Human Rights Commission. (2017). *Violence against Women in Australia: Australian Human Rights Commission Submission to the Special Rapporteur on Violence Against Women*, www.humanrights.gov.au/sites/default/files/AHRC_20170120_violence_against_women_submission.pdf.

Australian Institute of Health and Warfare. (2018). *Family, Domestic and Sexual Violence in Australia*, www.aihw.gov.au/getmedia/d1a8d479-a39a-48c1-bbe2-4b27c7a321e0/aihw-fdv-02.pdf.aspx?inline=true.

Badinter, Elisabeth. (1995). *XY: On Masculine Identity*. Trans. Lydia Davis. New York: Columbia University Press.

Bandura, Albert. (2016). *Moral Disengagement: How People do Harm and Live with Themselves*. New York: Worth Publishers.

Bang, Brandy, Paige L. Baker, Alexis Carpinteri, and Vincent B. Van Hasselt. (2014). *Commercial Sexual Exploitation of Children*. Cham: Springer.

Baral Stefan, Chris Beyrer, Kathryn Muessig, Tonia Potect, Andrea L. Wirtz, Michaele R. Decker, Susan G. Sherman, and Deanna Kerrigan. (2012). "Burden of HIV Among Female Sex Workers in Low-Income and Middle-Income Countries: A Systematic Review and Meta-Analysis." *Lancet Infectious Diseases* 12, no. 7: 538–49.

Barbagli, Marzio. (2015). *Farewell to the World: A History of Suicide*. Trans. Lucinda Byatt. Cambridge: Polity Press.

Barnes, Alan and Marcus Hearn. (1998). *Kiss Kiss Bang! Bang! The Unofficial James Bond Film Companion*. Woodstock: Overlook Press.

Baron, Cynthia. (1994). "*Doctor No*: Bonding Britishness to Racial Sovereignty." *Spectator* 14, no. 2: 68–81.

Barry, Brian. (2001). *Culture and Equality: An Egalitarian Critique of Multiculturalism*. Cambridge: Polity Press.

Bauböck, Rainer. (2005). *Citizenship Policies: International, State, Migrant and Democratic Perspectives*. Global Migration Perspectives 19. Geneva: Global Commission on International Migration.

Beck, Ulrich. (2002). "The Cosmopolitan Society and its Enemies." *Theory Culture & Society* 19, nos. 1–2: 17–44.

Bedoya, Nicolas. (2014, October 14). "Cartagena Beauty Queen Arrested in Child Sex Tourism Ring Bust." *Colombia Reports*, https://colombiareports.com/beauty-queen-among-five-arrested-cartagena-child-sex-tourism-ring-bust/.

Begel, Daniel and Antonia L. Baum. (2000). "The Athlete's Role." *Sport Psychiatry: Theory and Practice*. Ed. Daniel Begel and Robert W. Burton. New York: WW Norton. 45–58.

Belew, Christine M. (2010). "Killing One's Abuser: Premeditation, Pathology, or Provocation?" *Emory Law Journal* 59: 769.

Bellah, Robert N. (2002). "Seventy-Five Years." *South Atlantic Quarterly* 101, no. 2: 253–65.

Bello-Urrego, Alejandra del Rocío. (2013). "Sexo/género, violencias y derechos humanos: Perspectivas conceptuales para el abordaje de la violencia basada en género contra las mujeres desde el sector salud." *Revista Colombiana de Psiquiatría* 42, no. 1: 108–19.

Benedict, Jeffrey R. (1998). *Athletes and Acquaintance Rape*. Thousand Oaks: Sage.

Benhabib, Seyla. (2002). *The Claims of Culture: Equality and Diversity in the Global Era*. Princeton: Princeton University Press.

Benhabib, Seyla. (2011). *Dignity in Adversity: Human Rights in Troubled Times*. Cambridge: Polity Press.

Bennett, Barbara. (2016). "Dividing Women: The Framing of Trafficking for Sexual Exploitation in Magazines." *Feminist Media Studies* 16, no. 2: 205–22.

Bennett, Tony and Janet Woollacott. (1987). *Bond and Beyond: The Political Career of a Popular Hero*. Basingstoke: Macmillan.

Bensusan-Butt, David. (1941, August 18). *The Butt Report*, https://etherwave.files.wordpress.com/2014/01/butt-report-transcription-tna-pro-air-14-12182.pdf.

Bernal-Camargo, Diana Rocío, Antonio Varón-Mejía, Adriana Becerra-Barbosa, Kelly Chaib-De Mares, Enrique Seco-Martín, and Lorena Archila-Delgado. (2013). "Explotación sexual de niños, niñas y adolescentes: Modelo de intervención." *Revista Latinoamericana de Ciencias Sociales, Niñez y Juventud* 11, no. 2: 617–32.

Birley, Derek. (1995). *Playing the Game: Sport and British Society, 1910–45*. Manchester: Manchester University Press.

Black, Ann. (2019). "Cultural Expertise in Australia: Colonial Laws, Customs, and Emergent Legal Pluralism." *Cultural Expertise and Socio-Legal Studies* 78: 133–55.

Blair, J. Pete and Katherine W. Schweit. (2014). *A Study of Active Shooter Incidents, 2000–2013*. Texas State University and Federal Bureau of Investigation, U.S. Department of Justice, www.dm.usda.gov/ohsec/docs/FBI_Report_Active_Shooter_Study_2000_2013.pdf.

Blumer, Herbert. (1933). *Movies and Conduct*. New York: Macmillan.

Blumer, Herbert and Philip M. Hauser. (1933). *Movies, Delinquency and Crime*. New York: Macmillan.

Bodin, Jean. (1994). "Concerning the Citizen." *Citizenship*. Ed. Paul Barry Clarke. London: Pluto Press. 86–89.

Böhm, Robert, Hannes Rusch, and Özgür Gürerk. (2015). "What Makes People Go to War? Defensive Intentions Motivate Retaliatory and Preemptive Intergroup Aggression." *Evolution and Human Behavior* 37, no. 1: 29–34.

Bold, Christine. (1993). "'Under the Very Skirts of Britannia': Re-Reading Women in the James Bond Novels." *Queen's Quarterly* 100, no. 2: 310–27.

Bolívar, Simón. (2003). *El Libertador: Writings of Simón Bolívar.* Trans. Frederick H. Fornoff. Ed. David Bushnell. Oxford: Oxford University Press.

Bourdieu, Pierre. (1978). "Sport and Social Class." *Social Science Information* 17, no. 6: 819–40.

Boyer, Brandon. (2007, June 21). "Legacy Apologizes for *Law and Order* Crime Photo." *Gamasutra*, www.gamasutra.com/php-bin/news_index.php?story=14423.

Boyer, Marc. (2002). "El turismo en Europa, de la edad moderna al siglo XX." Trans. Carlos Larrinaga Rodríguez. *Historia Contemporánea* 25: 13–31.

Braudel, Fernand. (1984). *Civilization and Capitalism: 15th–18th Century, Volume III: The Perspective of the World.* Trans. Siân Reynolds. London: Collins.

Brecht, Bertolt. (1964). "Emphasis on Sport." *Brecht on Theatre.* Ed. John Willett. London: Macmillan. 6–9.

Breslau, K. (2008, May 15). "They Were Lying." *Newsweek.*

Britto, Lina. (2016). "Car Bombing Drug War History." *NACLA Report on the Americas* 48, no. 2: 177–80.

Brown, Chris. (2000). "Cultural Diversity and International Political Theory." *Review of International Studies* 26, no. 2: 199–213.

Brown, Wendy. (1988). *Manhood and Politics: A Feminist Reading in Political Theory.* Totowa: Rowman & Littlefield.

Brown, Wendy. (2010). *Walled States, Waning Sovereignty.* New York: Zone Books.

Buckingham, David. (2005). "A Special Audience? Children and Television." *A Companion to Television.* Ed. Janet Wasko. Malden: Blackwell. 468–86.

Bull, Hedley. (2002). *The Anarchical Society: A Study of Order in World Politics,* 3rd ed. New York: Columbia University Press.

Burke, Edmund. (1774). *Speech to the Electors of Bristol.* http://press-pubs.uchi cago.edu/founders/documents/v1ch13s7.html.

Burke, Edmund. (1994). "The Restraints on Men are Among Their Rights." *Citizenship.* Ed. Paul A. B. Clarke. London: Pluto Press. 121–23.

Burke, Marshall, Felipe González, Patrick Baylis, Sam Heft-Neal, Ceren Baysan, Sanjay Basu, and Solomon Hsiang. (2018). "Higher Temperatures Increase Suicide Rates in the United States and Mexico." *Nature Climate Change* 8: 723–29.

Butsch, Richard. (2000). *The Making of American Audiences: From Stage to Television, 1750–1990.* Cambridge: Cambridge University Press.

Butt, Nathalie, Frances Lambrick, Mary Menton, and Anna Renwick. (2019). "The Supply Chain of Violence." *Nature Sustainability* 2: 742–47.

Butterworth, Michael L. and Stormi D. Moskal. (2009). "American Football, Flags, and 'Fun': The Bell Helicopter Armed Forces Bowl and the Rhetorical Production of Militarism." *Communication, Culture & Critique* 2, no. 4: 411–33.

Cabañas, Miguel. (2012). "*Narcotelenovelas,* Gender, and Globalization in *Sin tetas no hay paraíso.*" *Latin American Perspectives* 39, no. 3: 74–87.

Cabral, Amilcar. (1973). *Return to the Source: Selected Speeches by Amilcar Cabral.* Africa Information Service ed. New York: Monthly Review Press.

Cabral, Amilcar. (1979). *Unity and Struggle: Speeches and Writings: Texts Selected by the PAIGC* [Partido Africano da Independência da Guiné e Cabo Verde]. Trans. Michael Wolfers. New York: Monthly Review Press.

Cain, Sian. (2019, May 30). "James Bond Still a Strong 'Recruitment Sergeant' for MI6, Says Expert." *Guardian*, www.theguardian.com/books/2019/may/30/james-bond-still-a-strong-recruitment-sergeant-for-mi6-says-expert.

Callaway, Annie. (2017). "Demand the Supply." *The Enough Project*, https://enough project.org/wp-content/uploads/2017/11/DemandTheSupply_EnoughProject_2017Rankings_final.pdf.

Camacho, Paul R. and William Locke Hauser. (2007). "Civil-Military Relations: Who Are the Real Principals? A Response to 'Courage in the Service of Virtue: The Case of General Shinseki's Testimony Before the Iraq War'." *Armed Forces & Society* 34, no. 1: 122–37.

Camacho Ordoñez, Leidy Bibiana and María Angélica Trujillo González. (2009). "La explotación sexual comercial infantil: Una ganancia subjetiva." *Revista Latinoamericana de Ciencias Sociales, Niñez y Juventud* 7, no. 2: 1009–25.

Camhaji, Elías. (2020, March 29). "'Vamos a saquearlo todo': Así operan los grupos que incitan a la rapiña por el coronavirus en México." *El País*, https://elpais.com/sociedad/2020-03-29/vamos-a-saquearlo-todo-asi-operan-los-grupos-que-incitan-a-la-rapina-por-el-coronavirus-en-mexico.html.

Canby, Vincent. (1971, December 18). "A Benign Bond." *New York Times*, www.nytimes.com/movie/review?res=950DE5D61038EF34BC4052DFB467838A669EDE&partner=Rotten%2520Tomatoes.

Carpiniello, Bernardo, Antonio Vita, and Claudia Mencacci. (2020). "Violence as a Social, Clinical, and Forensic Problem." *Violence and Mental Disorders*. Ed. Bernardo Carpiniello, Antonio Vita, and Claudia Mencacci. Cham: Springer. 3–24.

Carranza-Franco, Francy. (2019). *Demobilisation and Reintegration in Colombia: Building State and Citizenship*. London: Routledge.

Carras, Christi. (2019, November 13). "El Chapo's Wife Sparks Outrage with Upcoming Appearance on VH1's 'Cartel Crew'." *Los Angeles Times*, www.latimes.com/entertainment-arts/tv/story/2019-11-13/el-chapo-wife-cartel-crew-vh1-emma-coronel.

Caselli, Irene. (2016). "Soap Operas Get Whitewashed." *Index on Censorship* 45, no. 2: 74–77.

Castillo Murillejo, Norma Constanza and Nelson Enrique Rivera Reyes. (2013). "TICS, comunicación humana y violencia de género contra niños y adolescents víctimas de la explotación sexual comercial: Los casos de Bogotá y Cartagena, Colombia." *Actas – V Congreso Internacional Latina de Comunicación Social – V CILCS*, www.revistalatinacs.org/13SLCS/2013_actas/171_Castillo.pdf.

Cavanaugh, William T. (2009). *The Myth of Religious Violence: Secular Ideology and the Roots of Modern Conflict*. Oxford: Oxford University Press.

Centers for Disease Control. (2016). *Understanding School Violence Fact Sheet*, www.cdc.gov/violenceprevention/pdf/school_violence_fact_sheet-a.pdf.

Charles, Mathew. (2018, December 23). "Child Sex Trafficking Rife in Colombia's Picturesque Cartagena." *Guardian*, www.theguardian.com/global-development/2018/dec/23/child-sex-trafficking-rife-colombia-cartagena.

Charters, W. W. (1935). *Motion Pictures and Youth*. New York: Macmillan.

Chartier, Roger. (1989). "Texts, Printings, Readings." *The New Cultural History*. Ed. Lynn Hunt. Berkeley: University of California Press. 154–75.

Chartier, Roger. (2004). "Languages, Books and Reading from the Printed Word to the Digital Text." Trans. Teresa Lavender Fagan. *Critical Inquiry* 31, no. 1: 133–52.

Chartier, Roger. (2005a). "Crossing Borders in Early Modern Europe: Sociology of Texts and Literature." Trans. Maurice Elton. *Book History* 8: 37–50.

Chartier, Roger. (2005b, December 17). "Le droit d'auteur est-il une parenthèse dans l'histoire?" *Le Monde*, www.lemonde.fr/web/article/0,1-0,36-722516@45-1,0.html.

Chidester, Phillip J. (2009). "'The Toy Story of Life': Myth, Sport and the Mediated Reconstruction of the American Hero in the Shadow of the September 11th Terrorist Attacks." *Southern Communication Journal* 74, no. 4: 352–72.

Chua, Amy. (2003). *World on Fire: How Exporting Free Market Democracy Breeds Ethnic Hatred and Global Instability*. New York: Doubleday.

Chua, Amy. (2018). *Day of Empire: How Hyperpowers Rise to Global Dominance: And Why They Fall*. New York: Anchor.

"Church Says No, No to 'No'." (1965, May 19). *Los Angeles Times*.

Cockburn, Alexander and Jeffrey St. Clair. (1998). *White Out: The CIA, Drugs and the Press*. London: Verso.

Cole, Alyson M. (2008). "The Other V-Word: The Politics of Victimhood Fueling George W. Bush's War Machine." *Feminism and War: Confronting U.S. Imperialism*. Ed. Robin L. Riley, Chandra Talpade Mohanty, and Minnie Bruce Pratt. London: Zed Books. 117–30.

Collier, Robert. (2005, September 25). "Family Demands the Truth." *San Francisco Chronicle*, www.sfgate.com/news/article/FAMILY-DEMANDS-THE-TRUTH-New-inquiry-may-expose-2567400.php.

Colmenares, Germán. (1996). "La formación de la economía colonial (1500–1740)." *Historia económica de Colombia*. Ed. José Antonio Campo. Bogotá: Tercer Mundo Editores. 2–22.

Committee on the Elimination of All Forms of Discrimination Against Women. (2017). *Ninth Periodic Report of Colombia Under Article 18 of the Convention, Due in 2017*, CEDAW/C/COL/9.

Comstock, George. (1989). "Violence." *International Encyclopedia of Communications*, Vol. 4. Ed. Erik Barnouw, George Gerbner, Larry Gross, Wilbur Schramm, and Tobia L. Worth. New York: Oxford University Press. 289–94.

Comstock, George and Erica Scharrer. (1999). *Television: What's On, Who's Watching, and What It Means*. San Diego: Academic Press.

Connell, R. W. (1987). *Gender and Power: Society, the Person, and Sexual Politics*. Cambridge: Polity Press.

Connell, R. W. (1992). "A Very Straight Gay: Masculinity, Homosexual Experience, and the Dynamics of Gender." *American Sociological Review* 57, no. 6: 735–51.

Connell, R. W. (1998). "Masculinities and Globalization." *Men and Masculinities* 1, no. 1: 3–23.

Connell, R. W. (2001). *The Men and the Boys*. Berkeley: University of California Press.

Connell, R. W. (2003). *Masculinidades*. Mexico City: Programa Universitario de Estudios in Género, Universidad Nacional Autónoma de México.

Connell, R. W. (2005). *Masculinities*, 2nd ed. Berkeley: University of California Press.

Connolly, William E. (1993). *Political Theory and Modernity*. Ithaca: Cornell University Press.

Consejo Ciudadano Para La Seguridad Pública y La Justicia Penal AC. (2019). *Las 50 ciudades más violentas del mundo 2018*, http://seguridadjusticiaypaz.org.mx/files/estudio.pdf.

Cook, Philip and Conrad Heilmann. (2013). "Two Types of Self-Censorship: Public and Private." *Political Studies* 61, no. 1: 178–96.

Cooper, Cynthia A. (1996). *Violence on Television: Congressional Inquiry, Public Criticism and Industry Response: A Policy Analysis*. Lanham: University Press of America.

"Coronavirus: Crime Concerns as Disruption Widens." (2020, March 24). *BBC News*, www.bbc.com/news/uk-wales-52019550.

Coulter, Ann. (2004, December 29). "2004: Highlights and Lowlifes." *Ann Coulter*, www.anncoulter.com/columns/2004-12-29.html.

Council of Europe. (2019). *Democracy at Risk: Threats and Attacks against Media Freedom in Europe*, https://rm.coe.int/annual-report-2018-democracy-in-danger-threats-and-attacks-media-freed/1680926453.

Countercurrents Collective. (2020, March 19). "Coronavirus Pandemic: China and Cuba Send Medical Teams, Equipment and Medicine to Countries." *Pressenza*, www.pressenza.com/2020/03/coronavirus-pandemic-china-and-cuba-send-medical-teams-equipment-and-medicine-to-countries/.

Couric, Katie. (2008, May 4). "What Really Happened to Pat Tillman?" *CBSNews*, www.cbsnews.com/news/what-really-happened-to-pat-tillman/.

Cuartas, Jorge. (2018). "Physical Punishment against the Early Childhood in Colombia: National and Regional Prevalence, Sociodemographic Gaps, and Ten-Year Trends." *Children and Youth Services Review* 93: 428–40.

Cumings, Bruce. (2010). *The Korean War: A History*. New York: Modern Library.

Cunningham, Stuart. (1981). "The 'Force-Field' of Melodrama." *Quarterly Review of Film Studies* 6, no. 4: 347–64.

"A Cyber-House Divided." (2010, September 4). *Economist*: 61.

Dalberg, John Emerich Edward (Lord Acton). (1906). *Lectures on Modern History*. Ed. John Neville Figgis and Reginal Vere Laurence. London: Macmillan.

Dale, Edgar. (1933). *The Content of Motion Pictures*. New York: Macmillan.

Daubney, Martin. (2015, September 1). "James Bond: You're a Sexist, But We Love You for It." *Telegraph*, www.telegraph.co.uk/men/thinking-man/11836460/James-Bond-youre-a-sexist-but-we-love-you-for-it.html.

Davis, Angela Y. (2003). *Are Prisons Obsolete?* New York: Seven Stories Press.

De la Hoz Bohórquez, German Alberto and Jhon Henry Romero Quevedo. (2016). *Enterremos las armas para que florezca la Vida!!! Comportamiento del homicidio. Colombia, 2015*. Instituto Nacional de Medicina Legal y Ciencias Forenses, www.medicinalegal.gov.co/documents/88730/3418907/2.+HOMICIDIOS.pdf/70a4c34b-920c-465b-9902-936ffeab4afd.

Della Giusta, Marina, Maria Laura Di Tommaso, and Steinar Strøm. (2008). *Sex Markets: A Denied Industry*. London: Routledge.

de Nebrija, Antonio. (2016). "On Language and Empire: The Prologue to *Grammar of the Castilian Language* (1492)." Trans. Magalí Armillas-Tiseyra. *PMLA* 131, no. 1: 197–208.

Denning, Michael. (1992). "Licensed to Look: James Bond and the Heroism of Consumption." *Contemporary Marxist Literary Criticism*. Ed. Francis Mulhern. London: Longman. 211–29.

Densley, James A. and Jillian K. Peterson. (2017). *Gun Violence in America*. St. Paul: The Violence Project LLC.

de Pablos, Emiliano. (2019, January 21). "LatAm Scripted: The End of Telenovelas?" *Television Business International*, https://tbivision.com/2019/01/21/latin-american-scripted-raising-the-bar/.

de Pedro, Jesús Prieto. (1999). "Democracy and Cultural Difference in the Spanish Constitution of 1978." *Democracy and Ethnography: Constructing Identities in Multicultural Liberal States*. Ed. Carol J. Greenhouse and Roshanak Kheshti. Albany: State University of New York Press. 61–80.

Der Derian, James. (1992). *Antidiplomacy: Spies, Terror, Speed, and War*. Cambridge, MA: Blackwell.

Desli, Evangelia and Alexandra Gkoulgkoutsika. (2020). "Military Spending and Economic Growth: A Panel Data Investigation." *Economic Change and Restructuring*, https://doi.org/10.1007/s10644-020-09267-8.

de Sousa Santos, Bonaventura. (2007). *Democratizing Democracy: Beyond the Liberal Democratic Canon*. London: Verso.

Díaz Granados, Orlando Scoppetta D. and Rolando Rodríguez Cruz. (2006). "La explotación sexual de los niños en Cartagena de Indias y Bogotá, Colombia." *Revista Infancia Adolescencia y Familia* 1, no. 2: 247–58.

Díaz Nosty, Bernardo and Ruth A. de Frutos García. (2017). "Murders, Harassment and Disappearances: The Reality of Latin American Journalists in the XXI Century." *Revista Latina de Comunicación Social* 72: 1418–34.

Diss, Kathryn. (2020, March 28). "Preppers Were Considered Foolish Doomsayers before Coronavirus: Now They Feel Vindicated." *ABC News*, www.abc.net.au/news/2020-03-28/coronavirus-fears-see-americans-stockpile-guns/12088298.

Djellouli, Nehla and María Cristina Quevedo-Gómez. (2015). "Challenges to Successful Implementation of HIV and AIDS-Related Health Policies in Cartagena, Colombia." *Social Science & Medicine* 133: 36–44.

Dmowski, Seweryn. (2015). "Football Sites of Memory in the Eastern Bloc 1945–1991." *European Football and Collective Memory*. Ed. Wolfram Pyta and Nils Havermann. Houndmills: Palgrave Macmillan. 171–84.

Doughty, Steve. (2009, February 3). "Computers and TV Blamed for Teenage Violence and Casual Sex." *Daily Mail*, www.dailymail.co.uk/news/article-1133707/Computers-TV-blamed-teenage-violence-casual-sex.html.

Doward, Jamie. (2019, December 28). "Domestic Violence Kills 15 Times as Many as Terrorism in Britain." *Guardian*, www.theguardian.com/society/2019/dec/28/domestic-violence-kills-15-times-as-many-as-terrorism-in-britain.

Downing, John and Charles Husband. (2005). *Representing "Race": Racisms, Ethnicities and Media*. London: Sage.

Drummond, Lee. (1986). "The Story of Bond." *Symbolizing America*. Ed. Hervé Varenne. Lincoln: University of Nebraska Press. 66–89.

Du Bois, W. E. Burghardt. (1917). "Of the Culture of White Folks." *Journal of Race Development* 7, no. 4: 434–47.

Du Bois, W. E. Burghardt. (1942). "A Chronicle of Race Relations." *Phylon* 3, no. 1: 66–86.

Duggan, Lisa. (2003). *The Twilight of Equality? Neoliberalism, Cultural Politics, and the Attack on Democracy*. Boston: Beacon Press.

Durkheim, Émile. (1961). "The Solidarity of Occupational Groups." *Theories of Society: Foundations of Modern Sociological Theory. Volume I*. Ed. Talcott Parsons, Edward Shils, Kaspar D. Naegle, and Jesse R. Pitts. New York: Free Press of Glencoe. 356–63.

Eco, Umberto. (1972). "The Myth of Superman." Trans. Nancy Chilton. *Diacritics* 2, no. 1: 14–22.

Eco, Umberto. (1995, June 22). "Ur-Fascism." *New York Review of Books*, www.nybooks.com/articles/1995/06/22/ur-fascism/.

Eco, Umberto and Oreste del Buono, eds. (1966). *The Bond Affair*. Trans. R. A. Dawnie. London: MacDonald.

Edwards, Frank, Hedwig Lee, and Michael Esposito. (2019). "Risk of Being Killed by Police Use of Force in the United States by Age, Race-Ethnicity, and Sex." *Proceedings of National Academy of Sciences* 116, no. 34: 16793–98.

Eisenhower, Dwight D. (1972). "Liberty is at Stake." *SuperState: Readings in the Military-Industrial Complex*. Ed. Herbert I. Schiller and Joseph F. Phillips. Urbana: University of Illinois Press. 29–34.

Eisenstein, Sergei. (1987). *Nonindifferent Nature*. Trans. Herbert Marshall and Roberta Reader. New York: Cambridge University Press.

Elias, Norbert. (1978). "On Transformations of Aggressiveness." *Theory and Society* 5, no. 2: 229–42.

Elias, Norbert and Eric Dunning. (1986). *Quest for Excitement: Sport and Leisure in the Civilizing Process*. Oxford: Basil Blackwell.

Eloranta, Jan. (2016). "Cliometric Approaches to War." *Handbook of Cliometrics*. Ed. Claude Diebolt and Michael Haupert. Berlin: Springer-Verlag. 563–86.

Enck, Paulina. (2019, July 22). "A Female 007 Leaves Bond Fans Shaken (Not Stirred), and for Good Reason." *The Federalist*, https://thefederalist.com/2019/07/22/a-female-007-leaves-bond-fans-shaken-not-stirred-and-for-good-reason/.

Engels, Federico. (1968). *Anti-Dühring: La subversión de la ciencia por el señor Eugen Dühring*. Trans. Manuel Sacristan Luzon. México: Editorial Grijalbo, S. A.

Enloe, Cynthia. (1983). *Does Khaki Become You?: The Militarisation of Women's Lives*. Boston: South End Press.

Epstein, Angela. (2017, August 16). "I Hate to Admit It, but Women Pilots Make Me Nervous." *Daily Mail*, www.dailymail.co.uk/femail/article-4797202/I-hate-admit-women-pilots-make-nervous.html.

Erika, Sabine. (1986). "Nationalism and Women." *Politics* 21, no. 1: 82–88.

Espinosa Pezzia, Agustín, Alessandro Soares Da Silva, Carlos Contreras Ibáñez, Rosa María Cueto, Aldo García Rengifo, Fabio Ortolano, Juan Valencia, and Ángela Vera Ruíz. (2017). "Identidad nacional y sus relaciones con la ideología y el bienestar en cinco países de América Latina." *Avances en Psicología Latinoamericana* 35, no. 2: 351–74.

Evans, Robert. (2012, March 8). "Islamic States, Africans Walk Out on UN Gay Panel." *Reuters Africa*, http://af.reuters.com/article/topNews/idAFJOE82702T20120308?sp=true.

Evens, Tom and Katrien Lefever. (2011). "Watching the Football Game: Broadcasting Rights for the European Digital Television Market." *Journal of Sport & Social Issues* 35, no. 1: 33–49.

FAIR. (2005, March 21). *Counting the Iraqi Dead*, https://fair.org/take-action/action-alerts/counting-the-iraqi-dead/.

Falk, Richard A. (2004). *The Declining World Order: America's Imperial Geopolitics*. New York: Routledge.

Fanon, Frantz. (2004). *The Wretched of the Earth*. Trans. Richard Philcox. New York: Grove Press.

Farnsworth-Alvear, Ann, Marco Palacios, and Ana María Gómez López, eds. (2017). *The Colombia Reader: History, Culture, Politics*. Durham: Duke University Press.

Fazel, Seena, E. Naomi Smith, Zheng Chang, and John Richard Geddes. (2018). "Risk Factors for Interpersonal Violence: An Umbrella Review of Meta-Analyses." *British Journal of Psychiatry* 213: 609–14.

Federal Trade Commission. (2009). *Marketing Violent Entertainment to Children: A Sixth Follow-up Review of Industry Practices in the Motion Picture, Music Recording & Electronic Game Industries*, www.ftc.gov/sites/default/files/documents/reports/marketing-violent-entertainment-children-sixth-follow-review-industry-practices-motion-picture-music/p994511violententertainment.pdf.

Feinman, Ilene Rose. (2000). *Citizenship Rites: Feminist Soldiers & Feminist Antimilitarists*. New York: New York University Press.

Ferri, Pablo. (2020, April 2). "México vive su mes más violento pese a la pandemia." *El País*, https://elpais.com/internacional/2020-04-02/mexico-vive-su-mes-mas-violento-pese-a-la-pandemia.html.

Ferrier, Michelle. (2019). *Attacks and Harassment: The Impact on Female Journalists and Their Reporting*. Troll-Busters and International Women's Media Foundation, https://16dayscampaign.org/wp-content/uploads/2019/03/Attacks-and-Harassment-PDF.pdf.

Finkel, David. (2009). *The Good Soldiers*. New York: Farrar, Strauss and Giroux.

Finlay, Christopher. (2019). *Is Just War Possible?* Cambridge: Polity Press.

Fish, Mike. (2006). "E-Ticket: An Un-American Tragedy." *ESPN*, www.espn.com/espn/eticket/story?page=tillmanpart1.

Fleming, Ian. (1966). *Casino Royale*. London: Pan.

Fleming, Ian, and Raymond Chandler. (2014). "'You Want Me to Describe How It's Done?'" *Five Dials* 7: 30–33.

Florida, Richard. (2009). *Who's Your City? How the Creative Economy Is Making Where to Live the Most Important Decision of Your Life*. New York: Basic Books.

Florida, Richard. (2012). *The Rise of the Creative Class, Revisited*. New York: Basic Books.

Ford, Henry. (1929). *My Philosophy of Industry: An Authorized Interview by Ray Leone Faurote*. New York: Coward-McCann.

Forman, Henry James. (1933). *Our Movie Made Children*. New York: Macmillan.

Foucault, Michel. (1977). *Discipline and Punish: The Birth of the Prison*. Trans. Alan Sheridan. New York: Pantheon.

Foucault, Michel. (1978a). *The History of Sexuality, Vol. 1: An Introduction*. Trans. Robert Hurley. New York: Pantheon.

Foucault, Michel. (1978b). "About the Concept of the 'Dangerous Individual' in 19th Century Legal Psychiatry." Trans. Alain Baudot and Jane Couchman. *International Journal of Law and Psychiatry* 1: 1–18.

Foucault, Michel. (1980). *Power/Knowledge: Selected Interviews & Other Writings, 1972–1977*. Ed. Colin Gordon. New York: Pantheon.

Foucault, Michel. (1982). "The Subject and Power." Trans. Leslie Sawyer. *Critical Inquiry* 8, no. 4: 779–95.

Foucault, Michel. (1989). *Foucault Live: Collected Interviews 1961–1984*. Ed. Sylvère Lotringer. New York: Semiotext(e).

Foucault, Michel. (1991a). *The Foucault Effect: Studies in Governmentality*. Ed. Graham Burchell, Colin Gordon, and Peter Miller. Harlow: Harvester Wheatsheaf.

Foucault, Michel. (1991b). *Remarks on Marx: Conversations with Duccio Trombadori*. Trans. R. James Goldstein and James Cascaito. New York: Semiotext(e).

Foucault, Michel. (2000). *Power: Essential Works of Foucault 1954–1984 Volume Three*. Ed. James D. Faubion. New York: New Press.

Foucault, Michel. (2003a). *Abnormal: Lectures at the Collège de France 1974–1975*. Trans. Graham Burchell. Ed. Valerio Marchetti and Antonella Salomoni. New York: Picador.

Foucault, Michel. (2003b). *"Society Must Be Defended": Lectures at the Collège de France, 1975–1976*. Trans. David Macey. Ed. Mauro Bertani and Alessandro Fontana. New York: Picador.

Foucault, Michel. (2004). *Sécurité, territoire, population*. Paris: Seuil/Gallimard.

Foucault, Michel. (2006). *Psychiatric Power: Lectures at the Collège de France, 1973–74*. Trans. Graham Burchell. Ed. Jacques Lagrange. Basingstoke: Palgrave Macmillan.

Fox, Jonathan. (2002). "Ethnic Minorities and the Clash of Civilizations: A Quantitative Analysis of Huntington's Thesis." *British Journal of Political Science* 32, no. 3: 415–35.

Fox, William T. R. (1944). *The Super-Powers: The United States, Britain, and the Soviet Union–Their Responsibility for Peace*. New York: Harcourt Brace.

Franco, Jean. (2013). *Cruel Modernity*. Durham: Duke University Press.

Friera, S. (2004). "Auquel filósofo que escribía ajas llenas de herramientas." *Página 12*, www.pagina12.com.ar/diario/cultura/index-2004-06-25.html.

Fullerton, Jamie. (2018, January 7). "Suicide at Chinese iPhone Factory Reignites Concern Over Working Conditions." *Telegraph*, www.telegraph.co.uk/news/2018/01/07/suicide-chinese-iphone-factory-reignites-concern-working-conditions/.

Fundación Renacer. (2016). *Global Study on Sexual Exploitation of Children in Travel and Tourism Country-Specific Report: Colombia*, www.ecpat.org/wp-content/uploads/2016/10/3.-SECTT-COLOMBIA.pdf.

Galli, Cecilia. (2005, November 7). "Contra la tele basura." *Ciudad*.

Galtung, Johan. (1990). "Cultural Violence." *Journal of Peace Research* 27, no. 3: 291–305.

Garcia Canclini, Néstor. (2008). "Interview for the 9th Spanish Sociology Conference, 2007." Trans. Toby Miller. *Social Identities: Journal of Race, Nation and Culture* 14, no. 3: 389–94.

García Villegas, Mauricio. (2015, November 6). "Violentólogos." *El Espectador*, www.elespectador.com/opinion/opinion/violentologos-columna-597630.

Garfinkel, Harold. (1992). *Studies in Ethnomethodology*. Cambridge: Polity Press.

Garvey, Marcus. (2004). *Selected Writings and Speeches of Marcus Garvey*. Ed. Bob Blaisdell. New York: Dover.

Gaviria Castellanos, Jorge Luis, V. Gómez-Ortega, and P. Gutiérrez. (2015). "Quemaduras químicas por agresión: Caracteristicas e incidencia recogidas en el Hospital Simón Bolívar, Bogotá, Colombia." *Cirugía Plástica Ibero-Latinoamericana* 41, no. 1: 73–82.

Gearin, Mary and Ben Knight. (2020, March 29). "Family Violence Perpetrators Using COVID-19 as 'a Form of Abuse We Have Not Experienced Before'." *ABC News*, www.abc.net.au/news/2020-03-29/coronavirus-family-violence-surge-in-victoria/12098546.

Gellner, Ernest. (1988). *Plough, Sword and Book: The Structure of Human History*. Chicago: University of Chicago Press.

Gender Equality Observatory for Latin America and the Caribbean. (2019). *Measuring Femicide: Challenges and Efforts to Bolster the Process in Latin America and the Caribbean*, https://oig.cepal.org/sites/default/files/femicide_web.pdf?utm_source=CiviCRM&utm_medium=email&utm_campaign=20191125_oig_feminicide_en.

Gilliatt, Penelope. (1963, October 13). "Laughing It Off with Bond." *Observer*, www.mi6-hq.com/sections/articles/history_press_frwl_observer.php3?id=03595.

Gilligan, Carol. (1997, February 16). "A Therapist Examines the Hidden Problem of Male Depression." *New York Times Book Review*: 24.

Giraldo, Isis. (2015). "Machos y mujeres de armas tomar: Patriarcado y subjetividad feminina en la narco-telenovela colombiana contemporánea." *La Manzana de la Discordia* 10, no. 1: 67–81.

Girard, René. (1992). *Violence and the Sacred*. Trans. Patrick Gregory. Baltimore: The Johns Hopkins University Press.

Giulianotti, Richard. (1999). *Football: A Sociology of the Global Game*. Cambridge: Polity Press.

Global Burden of Disease 2016 Injury Collaborators. (2018). "Global Mortality from Firearms, 1990–2016." *Journal of the American Medical Association* 320, no. 8: 792–814.

Global Initiative to End All Corporal Punishment of Children. (2018, June). *Ending Family Violence in Colombia: Challenging Physical Punishment of Girls and Boys*, https://endcorporalpunishment.org/reports-on-every-state-and-territory/colombia/.

Global Witness. (2019). *Enemies of the State? How Governments and Business Silence Land and Environmental Defenders*, www.globalwitness.org/en/campaigns/environmental-activists/enemies-state/.

Goff, Stan. (2006, July 28). "Playing the Atheism Card against Pat Tillman's Family." *Truthdig*, www.truthdig.com/articles/playing-the-atheism-card-against-pat-tillmans-family/.

Gohdes, Anita R. and Sabine C. Carey. (2017). "Canaries in a Gold Mine? What the Killings of Journalists Tell Us About Future Repression." *Journal of Peace Research* 54, no. 2: 157–74.

Golding, William. (1954). *Lord of the Flies*. London: Faber and Faber.

Goldman, Emma. (1917). *Anarchism and Other Essays*, 3rd ed. New York: Mother Earth Publishing Association.

Gómez, Oscar A. and Des Gasper. (2013). *Human Security: A Thematic Guidance Note for Regional and National Human Development Report Teams*. United Nations Development Programme Human Development Report Office, http://hdl.handle.net/1765/50571.

González de Bustamante, Celeste and Jeannine E. Relly. (2016). "Professionalism Under Threat of Violence: Journalism, Reflexivity, and the Potential for Collective Professional Autonomy in Northern Mexico." *Journalism Studies* 17, no. 6: 684–702.

Gramlich, John. (2019, October 17). "5 Facts about Crime in the U.S." *Pew Research Center*, www.pewresearch.org/fact-tank/2019/10/17/facts-about-crime-in-the-u-s/.

Gramsci, Antonio. (1971). *Selections from the Prison Notebooks*. Trans. Quentin Hoare and Geoffrey Nowell-Smith. New York: International Publishers.

Gray, John. (2003). *Al Qaeda and What It Means to be Modern*. London: Faber and Faber.

Greenslade, Roy. (2003, February 17). "Their Master's Voice." *Guardian*, www.theguardian.com/media/2003/feb/17/mondaymediasection.iraq.

Greenwald, Glenn. (2007, April 25) "The Pat Tillman and Jessica Lynch Frauds." *Salon*, www.salon.com/2007/04/25/tillman_lynch/.

Grillo, Ioan. (2016). *Gangster Warlords: Drug Dollars, Killing Fields, and the New Politics of Latin America*. New York: Bloomsbury.

Grinshteyn, Eric and David Hemenway. (2016). "Violent Death Rates: The US Compared with Other High Income OECD Countries, 2010." *American Journal of Medicine* 129, no. 3: 266–73.

Gruffydd Jones, Branwen, ed. (2006). *Decolonizing International Relations*. Plymouth: Rowman & Littlefield.

Guattari, Pierre-Félix. (1996). *The Guattari Reader*. Ed. Gary Genosko. Oxford: Blackwell.

Guerrero, Linda. (2013). "Burns Due to Acid Assaults in Bogotá, Colombia." *Burns* 39, no. 5: 1018–23.

Guerrero, Rodrigo and Andrés Fandiño-Losada. (2017). "Is Colombia a Violent Country?" *Colombia Médica* 48, no. 1: 9–11.

Guerrero-Figueroa Guerrero, Guillermo. (2016). "Incidencias del ESCNNA (explotación sexual comercial de niños, niñas, y adolescentes) en el turismo." *Revista Adelante Ahead* 7, no. 1: 88–96.

Habermas, Jürgen. (2006). "Religion in the Public Sphere." *European Journal of Philosophy* 14, no. 1: 1–25.

Haggbloom, Steven J., Renee Warnick, Jason E. Warnick, Vinessa K. Jones, Gary L. Yarborough, Tenea M. Russell, Chris M. Borecky, Reagan McGahhey, John L. Powell III, Jamie Beavers, and Emmanuelle Monte. (2002). "The 100 Most

Eminent Psychologists of the 20th Century." *Review of General Psychology* 6, no. 2: 139–52.

Hall, Stuart. (1995). "Parties on the Verge of a Nervous Breakdown." *Soundings* 1: 19–33.

Hall, Stuart. (2010). *Sin garantías: Trayectorias y problemáticas en estudios culturales*. Ed. Eduardo Restrepo, Catherine Walsh, and Victor Vich. Popayán: Envión; Lima: Instituto de Estudios Peruanos; Bogotá: Instituto de Estudios Sociales y Culturales.

Hall, Stuart. (2016). *Cultural Studies 1983: A Theoretical History*. Ed. Jennifer Daryl Slack and Lawrence Grossberg. Durham: Duke University Press.

Halliday, Fred. (1990). "'The Sixth Great Power': On the Study of Revolution and International Relations." *Review of International Studies* 16, no. 3: 207–21.

Halliday, Fred. (2001). *The World at 2000: Perils and Promises*. Basingstoke: Palgrave.

Halliday, Fred. (2004, September 15). "The Crisis of Universalism: America and Radical Islam After 9/11." *OpenDemocracy*, www.opendemocracy.net/en/article_2092jsp/.

Hammad, Hannah. (2019, February 8). "Detainment: True Crime Is Popular but Here's Why James Bulger Film Has Upset So Many People." *The Conversation*, http://theconversation.com/detainment-true-crime-is-popular-but-heres-why-james-bulger-film-has-upset-so-many-people-111441.

Han, Byung-Chul. (2018). *Topology of Violence*. Trans. Amanda DeMarco. Cambridge, MA: MIT Press.

Hanchard, Michael. (2018). *The Spectre of Race: How Discrimination Haunts Western Democracy*. Princeton: Princeton University Press.

Hansen, Susan, Alec McHoul, Mark Rapley, Hayley Miller, and Toby Miller. (2003). *Beyond Help: A Consumer's Guide to Psychology*. Ross-on-Wye: PCCS Books.

Hardt, Michael and Antonio Negri. (2000). *Empire*. Cambridge, MA: Harvard University Press.

Harris, Marvin. (1991). *Cannibals and Kings: The Origins of Cultures*. New York: Vintage.

Harvey, David. (2003). *The New Imperialism*. Oxford: Oxford University Press.

Hawkins, Darnell F. (2003). "Editor's Introduction." *Violent Crime: Assessing Race and Ethnic Differences*. Ed. Darnell F. Hawkins. New York: Cambridge University Press. xiii–xxv.

Healy, Gene. (2004, May 7). "You Gotta Serve Somebody." *Cato*.

Hearn, Jeff. (2012, May 23). "The 'Missing' Men of International Relations." *E-International Relations*, www.e-ir.info/2012/05/23/the-missing-men-of-international-relations/.

Hegel, Georg Wilhelm Friedrich. (2001). *The Philosophy of History*. Trans. J. Sibree. Kitchener: Batoche Books.

Hegel, Georg Wilhelm Friedrich. (2008). *Reading Hegel: The Introductions*. Ed. Aakash Singh and Rimina Mohapatra. Melbourne: re.press.

Hellman, Geoffrey T. (1962, April 21). "Bond's Creator." *New Yorker*: 32.

Helmore, Edward. (2019, December 28). "2019 Saw Most Mass Killings on Record, US Database Reveals." *Guardian*, www.theguardian.com/us-news/2019/dec/28/mass-killings-2019-us-database.

Herder, Johann Gottfried von. (2002). *Philosophical Writings*. Trans. and Ed. Michael N. Forster. Cambridge: Cambridge University Press.

Herman, Edward S. (2004). "Selective Information is Misinformation." *Democratic Communiqué* 19: 1–12.

Herrero, Juan, Francisco J. Rodríguez, and Andrea Torres. (2017). "Acceptability of Partner Violence in 51 Societies: The Role of Sexism and Attitudes Towards Violence in Social Relationships." *Violence against Women* 23, no. 3: 351–67.

Hersh, Seymour. (2004, April 30). "Torture at Abu Ghraib." *New Yorker*, www.newyorker.com/magazine/2004/05/10/torture-at-abu-ghraib.

Hobbes, Thomas. (1640). *The Elements of Law Natural and Politic*, http://socserv2.socsci.mcmaster.ca/~econ/ugcm/3ll3/hobbes/elelaw.

Hobbes, Thomas. (1651). *Leviathan or the Matter, Forme, & Power of a Commonwealth Ecclesiasticall and Civil*. London: Andrew Crooke.

Hobsbawm, Eric. (1995). *The Age of Extremes: The Short Twentieth Century, 1914–1991*. London: Michael Joseph.

Hobsbawm, Eric. (1998). "The Nation and Globalization." *Constellations* 5, no. 1: 1–9.

Hobsbawm, Eric and Terence Ranger, eds. (2002). *La invención de la tradición*. Trans. Omar Rodríguez. Barcelona: Editorial Crítica.

Hobson, J. A. (1902). *Imperialism: A Study*. London: James Nisbet & Co.

Hodge, Bob and David Tripp. (1986). *Children and Television*. Cambridge: Polity Press.

Hoggart, Richard. (1965). "The World We Offer." *Health Education Journal* 23: 34–40.

Høiby, Marte and Rune Ottosen, eds. (2015). *Journalism Under Pressure: A Mapping of Editorial Policies for Journalists Covering Conflict*. Oslo: Høgskolen i Oslo og Akershus.

Horkheimer, Max. (2013). *Eclipse of Reason*. London: Bloomsbury.

Houlihan, Barrie. (1997). *Sport, Policy and Politics: A Comparative Analysis*. London: Routledge.

Howard, Michael. (1984). "The Causes of Wars." *The Wilson Quarterly* 8, no. 3: 90–103.

Howden, Daniel, David Hardaker, and Stephen Castle. (2006, February 10). "How a Meeting of Leaders in Mecca Set Off the Cartoon Wars Around the World." *Independent*, www.independent.co.uk/news/world/middle-east/how-a-meeting-of-leaders-in-mecca-set-off-the-cartoon-wars-around-the-world-6109473.html.

Hsiang, Solomon, Marshall Burke, and Edward Miguel. (2013). "Quantifying the Influence of Climate on Human Conflict." *Science* 341, no. 6151, https://science.sciencemag.org/content/341/6151/1235367.

Huertas, Omar Díaz and Nayibe Jiménez Rodríguez. (2016). "Feminicidio en Colombia: Reconocimiento de fenómeno social a delito." *Pensamiento Americano* 9, no. 16: 110–20.

Human Rights Watch. (2019). *Submission by Human Rights Watch to the Committee on the Elimination of All Forms of Discrimination against Women on Colombia*, www.hrw.org/news/2019/02/01/submission-human-rights-watch-committee-elimination-all-forms-discrimination-against.

Hume, David. (1996). *Essays on Suicide and Immortality of the Soul.* N. p.: Infomotions.

Hunter, Alan. (2009). "Soft Power: China on the Global Stage." *Chinese Journal of International Politics* 2, no. 3: 373–98.

Huntington, Samuel. (1993). "The Clash of Civilizations?" *Foreign Affairs* 72, no. 3: 22–28.

"If a 13-Year Old Murders a Ten-Year-Old is it a Crime?" (2019, November 5). *The Economist,* www.economist.com/graphic-detail/2019/11/05/if-a-13-year-old-murders-a-ten-year-old-is-it-a-crime.

Institute for Economics & Peace. (2017). *Global Terrorism Index: Measuring and Understanding the Impact of Terrorism,* http://globalterrorismindex.org/.

Institute for Economics & Peace. (2018). *Índice de datos sobre homicidios. Resultados 2018: ¿Como registramos los homicidios en México?* http://economicsandpeace.org/wp-content/uploads/2018/08/Indice-de-Datos-sobre-Homicidios-2018.pdf.

Institute for Economics & Peace. (2019). *Global Peace Index 2019,* http://visionofhumanity.org/app/uploads/2019/07/GPI-2019web.pdf.

Instituto Colombiano de Medicina Legal. (2015). *Forensis, datos para la vida,* www.medicinalegal.gov.co/documents/88730/1656998/Forensis+Interactivo+2014.24-JULpdf.pdf/9085ad79-d2a9-4c0d-a17b-f845ab96534b.

Instituto Nacional de Estadística y Geografía. (2018). *Encuesta Nacional de Victimización y Percepción sobre Seguridad Pública (ENVIPE) 2018: Principales Resultados,* http://internet.contenidos.inegi.org.mx/contenidos/Productos/prod_serv/contenidos/espanol/bvinegi/productos/nueva_estruc/702825104795.pdf.

International Federation of Journalists. (2019). *In the Shadow of Violence: Journalists and Media Staff Killed in 2018,* www.ifj.org/fileadmin/user_upload/IFJ_2018_Killed_Report_FINAL_pages.pdf.

Intimations–A Question of Influences. (1966). "Malcolm Muggeridge and John le Carré." Produced by Margaret McCall. *BBC,* www.bbc.co.uk/iplayer/episode/p00nw1tb/intimations-10-john-le-carre#.

Irigaray, Luce. (2004). *Luce Irigaray: Key Writings.* Ed. Luce Irigaray. New York: Continuum.

"Irresponsible Athletes." (1998, May 6). *New York Times*: A22.

Jackson, Matthew O. and Massimo Morelli. (2011). "The Reasons for Wars: An Updated Survey." *The Handbook on the Political Economy of War.* Ed. Christopher J. Coyne and Rachel L. Mathers. Cheltenham: Edward Elgar Publishing. 34–57.

Jaggi, Maya. (2000, October 21). "Bhikhu Parekh: First Among Equalisers." *Guardian*: 6.

"James Bond vs. Saddam Hussein." (1998, February 27). *New York Times*: A24.

"James Bulger Killer Jon Venables Jailed Over Indecent Images." (2018, February 7). *BBC News,* www.bbc.com/news/uk-england-42972085.

Jarvie, Grant and Joseph Maguire. (1994). *Sport and Leisure in Social Thought.* London: Routledge.

Jashinsky, Jared, Scott H. Burton, Carl L. Hanson, Josh West, Christopher Giraud-Carrier, Michael Dean Barnes, and Trenton Argyle. (2014). "Tracking Suicide Risk Factors Through Twitter in the US." *Crisis* 35, no. 1: 51–59.

Jeffreys-Jones, Rhodri. (1989). *The CIA & American Democracy*. New Haven: Yale University Press.

Jenke, Libby and Christopher Gelpi (2017). "Theme and Variations: Historical Contingencies in the Causal Model of Interstate Conflict." *Journal of Conflict Resolution* 61, no. 10: 2262–84.

Jerryson, Michael, Mark Juergensmeyer, and Margo Kitts, eds. (2013). *The Oxford Handbook of Religion and Violence*. New York: Oxford University Press.

Johnson, Jake. (2020, April 6). "Trump Refuses to Allow Dr. Fauci to Answer Question on Dangers of Hydroxychloroquine." *CommonDreams*, www.common dreams.org/news/2020/04/06/really-chilling-moment-trump-refuses-allow-dr-fauci-answer-question-dangers.

Johnson, Loch K. (1996). *Secret Agencies: U.S. Intelligence in a Hostile World*. New Haven: Yale University Press.

Joyce, James. (2000). *Ulysses*. Ed. Declan Kiberd. London: Penguin.

Judd, Jackie. (2001, May 31). "Army Engineers Come up with New Combat Vehicle Inspired by James Bond Films." *Morning Edition, National Public Radio*.

Jungblut, Marc and Abit Hoxha. (2016). "Conceptualizing Journalistic Self-Censorship in Post-Conflict Societies: A Qualitative Perspective on the Journalistic Perception of News Production in Serbia, Kosovo, and Macedonia." *Media, War and Conflict* 10, no. 2: 222–38.

Kaldor, Mary. (2012). *New and Old Wars: Organised Violence in a Global Era*, 3rd ed. Cambridge: Polity Press.

Kant, Immanuel. (1991). *Political Writings*, 2nd ed. Trans. H. B. Nisbet. Ed. Hans Reiss. Cambridge: Cambridge University Press.

Kant, Immanuel. (2006). *Toward Perpetual Peace and Other Writings on Politics, Peace, and History*. Trans. D. L. Colclasure. Ed. P. Kleingeld. New Haven: Yale University Press.

Kara, Siddharth. (2018, October 12). "Is Your Phone Tainted by the Misery of 35,000 Children in Congo's Mines?" *Guardian*, www.theguardian.com/global-development/2018/oct/12/phone-misery-children-congo-cobalt-mines-drc.

Keane, John. (2004). *Violence and Democracy*. Cambridge: Cambridge University Press.

Keefe, Patrick R. (2010). "Privatized Spying: The Emerging Intelligence Industry." *The Oxford Handbook of National Security Intelligence*. Ed. Loch K. Johnson. Oxford: Oxford University Press. 296–309.

Kennedy, John F. (1960, December 26). "The Soft American." *Sports Illustrated*, www.artofmanliness.com/articles/jfk-on-the-dangers-of-americans-getting-soft/.

Kennedy, John N. (2019, November 14). *Sen. John Kennedy (R-La.) Urges VH1 to Cancel Television Series Glorifying Work of Drug Cartels*, www.kennedy.senate.gov/public/press-releases?ID=F28CBCE7-2C4F-423E-A934-0666AAC1F730.

Keynes, John Maynard. (1936). *The General Theory of Employment, Interest and Money*. London: Palgrave Macmillan.

Kidd, Benjamin. (2009). *Social Evolution*. Cambridge: Cambridge University Press.

Kiesling, Barrett C. (1937). *Talking Pictures: How They are Made How to Appreciate Them*. Richmond: Johnson Publishing.

Kim, Hun Shik. (2010). "Forces of Gatekeeping and Journalists' Perceptions of Physical Danger in Post-Saddam Hussein's Iraq." *Journalism and Mass Communication Quarterly* 87, no. 3–4: 484–500.

Knight, Malcolm, Norman Loayza, and Delano Villanueva. (1996). "The Peace Dividend: Military Spending Cuts and Economic Growth." World Bank Policy Research Working Paper 1577, http://documents.worldbank.org/curated/en/1549 41468766463442/107507322_20041117142015/additional/multi0page.pdf.

Kollontai, Alexandra. (1978). *Selected Writings of Alexandra Kollontai*. Trans. Alix Holt. Westport: Lawrence Hill and Company.

Koren, Marina. (2020, April 2). "The Pandemic Is Turning the Natural World Upside Down." *The Atlantic*, www.theatlantic.com/science/archive/2020/04/coronavirus-pandemic-earth-pollution-noise/609316/?utm_source=facebook&utm_medium=social&utm_campaign=share.

Krakauer, Jon. (2009). *When Men Win Glory: The Odyssey of Pat Tillman*. New York: Doubleday.

Kraus, Hans and Ruth P. Hirschland. (1953). "Muscular Fitness and Health." *Journal of the American Association for Health, Physical Education, and Recreation* 24, no. 10: 17–19.

Krauze, Enrique. (1994, June 28). "México en un balón." *El País*, http://elpais.com/diario/1994/06/28/opinion/772754409_850215.html.

Kristeva, Julia. (1993). *Nations Without Nationalism*. Trans. Leon S. Roudiez. New York: Columbia University Press.

Kristeva, Julia. (1997). *The Portable Kristeva*. Ed. Kelly Oliver. New York: Columbia University Press.

Kusz, Kyle W. (2007). "From NASCAR Nation to Pat Tillman: Notes on Sport and the Politics of White Cultural Nationalism in Post-9/11 America." *Journal of Sport & Social Issues* 31, no. 1: 77–88.

Kymlicka, Will. (1995). *Multicultural Citizenship: A Liberal Theory of Minority Rights*. Oxford: Oxford University Press.

Laidlaw, S. and M. Mendoza. (2007, August 4). "General Suspected Cause of Tillman Death." *Washington Post*, www.washingtonpost.com/wpdyn/content/article/2007/08/03/AR2007080301868.html.

Langton, Lynn and Jennifer Truman. (2014, September). *Socio-Emotional Impact of Violent Crime*. U.S. Department of Justice, Office of Justice Programs, Bureau of Justice Statistics, www.bjs.gov/content/pub/pdf/sivc.pdf.

Laqua, Daniel. (2011). "Intellectual Cooperation, the League of Nations, and the Problem of Order." *Journal of Global History* 6, no. 2: 223–47.

Larraín, América. (2015). "Bailar fútbol: Reflexiones sobre el cuerpo y la nación en Colombia." *Boletín de Antropología* 30, no. 50: 191–207.

Lasch, Christopher. (1979). *The Culture of Narcissism: American Life in an Age of Diminishing Expectations*. New York: Warner.

Latour, Bruno. (1993). *We Have Never Been Modern*. Trans. Catherine Porter. Cambridge, MA: Harvard University Press.

Laudati, Ann and Charlotte Mertens. (2019). "Resources and Rape: Congo's (Toxic) Discursive Complex." *African Studies Review* 62, no. 4: 57–82.

Leaños, John. (2005). "Intellectual Freedom and Pat Tillman." *Bad Subjects*.

Le Bon, Gustave. (1899). *Psychologie des Foules*. Paris: Alcan.

Lee, Bandy X. (2019). *Violence: An Interdisciplinary Approach to Causes, Consequences, and Cures*. Hoboken: Blackwell.

Lee, Sang Yup. (2020). "Do Effects of Copycat Suicides Vary with the Reasons for Celebrity Suicides Reported by the Media?" *The Social Science Journal*, www.tandfonline.com/doi/abs/10.1016/j.soscij.2019.03.003.

Влади́мир Ильи́ч Ле́нин. [Lenin, V. I.]. (2014). *State and Revolution*. Chicago: Haymarket Books.

Lennon, John. (1971, January 21). "Interview with Tariq Ali and Robin Blackburn." *Red Mole*, www.beatlesinterviews.org/db1971.0121.beatles.html.

Levy, Jack S. (1998). "The Causes of War and the Conditions of Peace." *Annual Review of Political Science* 1: 139–65.

Lewis, Bernard. (1990, September). "The Roots of Muslim Rage: Why So Many Muslims Deeply Resent the West, and Why Their Bitterness Will Not Be So Easily Mollified." *Atlantic Monthly*: 47–58.

Lincoln, Abraham. (1838, January 27). *The Perpetuation of Our Political Institutions: Address Before the Young Men's Lyceum of Springfield, Illinois*, www.abrahamlincolnonline.org/lincoln/speeches/lyceum.htm.

Lippmann, Walter. (1982). *The Essential Lippmann: A Political Philosophy for Liberal Democracy*. Ed. Clinton Rossiter and James Lare. Cambridge, MA: Harvard University Press.

Lipsyte, Robert. (2011, January 30). "You Must Watch the Empire Bowl." *TomDispatch*, www.tomdispatch.com/archive/175348.

Lisle, Debbie. (2016). *Holidays in the Danger Zone: Entanglements of War and Tourism*. Minneapolis: University of Minnesota Press.

Lister, Ruth. (1997). "Dialectics of Citizenship." *Hypatia* 12: 6–21.

Locke, John. (1997). *Political Essays*. Ed. Mark Goldie. Cambridge: Cambridge University Press.

Lockford, Lesa. (2008). "Investing in the Political Beyond." *Qualitative Inquiry* 14, no. 1: 3–12.

Löfgren Nilsson, Monica and Henrik Örnebring. (2016). "Journalism Under Threat." *Journalism Practice* 10, no. 7: 880–90.

Londoño, Nora H., Diana Valencia, Mario García, and Catalina Restrepo. (2014). "Factores causales de la explotación sexual infantil en niños, niñas y adolescentes en Colombia." *El Ágora USB Medellín-Colombia* 15, no. 1: 241–54.

Ло́тман, Ю́рий Миха́йлович [Lotman, Yuri]. (2004). *Culture and Explosion*. Trans. Wilma Clark. Ed. Marina Grishakova. Berlin: Mouton de Gruyter.

Luhmann, Niklas. (2013). *Theory of Society*, Vol. 2. Trans. Rhodes Barrett. Stanford: Stanford University Press.

Lukács, György. (1972). *History and Class Consciousness: Studies in Marxist Dialectics*. Trans. Rodney Livingstone. Cambridge, MA: MIT Press.

Luxemburg, Rosa. (1986). *Rosa Luxemburg Speaks*. Ed. Mary-Alice Waters. New York: Pathfinder Press.

Luxemburg, Rosa. (2004). *The Rosa Luxemburg Reader*. Ed. Peter Hudis and Kevin B. Anderson. New York: Monthly Review Press.

Lynd, Robert S. and Helen Merrell Lynd. (1956). *Middletown: A Study in Modern American Culture.* New York: Harcourt, Brace and Company.

Lyotard, Jean-François. (1993). *Political Writings.* Trans. B. Readings with K. P. Geiman. London: UCL Press.

Machiavelli, Niccolò. (1950). *The Prince and the Discourses.* Ed. Christian E. Detmold and Luigi Ricci, rev. E. R. P. Vincent. New York: Modern Library.

Machiavelli, Niccolò. (1520). *The Seven Books on the Art of War.* Trans. Henry Neville, www.marxists.org/reference/archive/machiavelli/works/art-war/index.htm.

Macintyre, Alasdair. (2007). *After Virtue: A Study in Moral Theory,* 3rd ed. Notre Dame: University of Notre Dame Press.

Mackie, Vera. (2012). "The 'Afghan Girls': Media Representations and Frames of War." *Continuum: Journal of Media & Cultural Studies* 26, no. 1: 115–31.

Mahmud, Tayyab. (1997). "Migration, Identity, & the Colonial Encounter." *Oregon Law Review* 76, no. 3: 633–90.

Mahmud, Tayyab. (1999). "Colonialism and Modern Constructions of Race: A Preliminary Inquiry." *University of Miami Law Review* 53, no. 4: 1219–46.

Malcolm X. (2011). *The End of White Supremacy: Four Speeches.* New York: Arcade Publishing.

Malthus, Thomas Robert. (1836). *Principles of Political Economy.* London: W. Pickering.

Mandel, Ernest. (1976). *Late Capitalism.* Trans. Joris De Bres. London: NLB.

Mandel, Ernest. (1984). *Delightful Murder: A Social History of the Crime Story.* London: Pluto Press.

Mannheim, Karl. (2017). *From Karl Mannheim,* 2nd ed. Ed. Kurt H. Wolff. London: Routledge.

毛泽东 [Mao Zedong]. (1971). *Selected Readings from the Works of Mao Zedong.* Ed. Editorial Committee for Selected Readings from the Work of Mao Tsetung. Beijing: Foreign Languages Press.

Marconi, Guglielmo. (1924). "Foreword." *The Story of Broadcasting.* A. R. Burrows. London: Cassell. Vii.

Marcos, Ana. (2018, September 3). "Why Pablo Escobar Is Anything but Cool." *El País,* https://elpais.com/elpais/2018/08/31/inenglish/1535708632_118999.html.

Marcuse, Herbert. (1977). "Murder Is Not a Political Weapon." Trans. Jeffrey Herf. *New German Critique* 12: 7–8.

Marcuse, Herbert. (2009). *Negations: Essays in Critical Theory.* Trans. and Ed. Jeremy J. Shapiro. London: MayFlyBooks.

Martín-Barbero, Jesús. (2004). "Nuestra excéntrica y heterogénea modernidad." *Estudios Políticos* 25: 115–34.

Martín-Baró, Ignacio. (1998). *Psicología de la liberación.* Ed. Amalio Blanco. Madrid: Editorial Trotta.

Martínez, Marcos. (2019, May 6). "Mexico's Amlo Riding High 10 Months After Election." *BBC News,* www.bbc.com/news/world-latin-america-47946959.

Martinson, Jane. (2012, October 30). "Is *Skyfall* a Less Sexist Bond Film?" *Guardian,* www.theguardian.com/film/the-womens-blog-with-jane-martinson/2012/oct/30/skyfall-less-sexist-bond-film.

Marvin, Carolyn. (1988). *When Old Technologies Were New: Thinking about Electronic Communication in the Late Nineteenth Century*. New York: Oxford University Press.

Marx, Karl and Frederick Engels. (2006). *Communist Manifesto*. Trans. Helen Macfarlane. Ed. Frederick Engels. Mountain View: New York Labor News.

"Mary Tillman, Mother of Slain Army Ranger and Former NFL Star Pat Tillman, on Her Four-Year Quest to Expose the Military Cover-Up of Her Son's Death by Members of His Own Unit." (2008, May 22). *Democracy Now!*, www.democracynow.org/2008/5/22/mary_tillman_mother_of_slain_nfl.

Marzullo, Michelle A. and Alyn J. Libman. (2009). *Hate Crimes and Violence against Lesbian, Gay, Bisexual and Transgender People*. Ed. Ché Juan Gonzales Ruddell-Tabisola. Washington: Human Rights Campaign Foundation.

Masucci, Madeline and Lynn Langton. (2017). *Hate Crime Victimization, 2004–2015*. Special Report NCJ 250653. U.S. Department of Justice, Office of Justice Programs, Bureau of Justice Statistics.

May, Mark A. and Frank K. Shuttleworth. (1933). *The Social Conduct and Attitudes of Movie Fans*. New York: Macmillan.

May, Theresa. (2016). *Theresa May Attacks "Freedom of Movement" Culture*, www.youtube.com/watch?v=pcbf6vMDlF0.

Mazrui, Ali A. (2014). *Resurgent Islam and the Politics of Identity*. Ed. Ramzi Badran and Thomas Uthup. Newcastle: Cambridge Scholars Publishing.

Mazzucato, Mariana. (2015). *The Entrepreneurial State: Debunking Public vs. Private Sector Myths*. New York: Public Affairs.

Mbembe, Achille. (2003). "Necropolitics." Trans. Libby Meintjes. *Public Culture* 15, no. 1: 11–40.

McAllister, D. C. (2017, July 24). "Why James Bond Should Never Be a Woman." *The Federalist*, http://thefederalist.com/2017/07/24/james-bond-never-woman/.

McAnally, Helena M., Lindsay A. Robertson, Victor C. Strasburger, and Robert J. Hancox. (2013). "Bond, James Bond: A Review of 46 Years of Violence in Films." *Archives of Pediatrics & Adolescent Medicine* 167, no. 2: 195–96.

McCain, John. (2004, May 4). "Courage and Honor: Remembering Pat Tillman." *National Review*, www.nationalreview.com/2004/05/courage-and-honor-nro-primary-document/.

McCarthy, Todd. (1995, November 15). "Goldeneye." *Variety*, https://variety.com/1995/film/reviews/goldeneye-1200443796/.

McDonagh, Maitland. (1995). "Goldeneye." *TV Guide*, www.tvguide.com/movies/goldeneye/review/130384/.

McHugh, Kathleen Anne. (1999). *American Domesticity: From How-To Manual to Hollywood Melodrama*. New York: Oxford University Press.

McKay, Jim. (2018). *Transnational Tourism Experiences at Gallipoli*. Singapore: Springer.

McMahon, Susan D., Samantha Reaves, Elizabeth A. McConnell, Eric Peist, Linda Ruiz, and the APA Task Force on Classroom Violence Directed Against Teachers. (2017). "The Ecology of Teachers' Experiences with Violence and Lack of Administrative Support." *American Journal of Community Psychology* 60, nos. 3–4: 502–15.

McMichael, Philip. (1996). *Development and Social Change: A Global Perspective.* Thousand Oaks: Pine Forge Press.

Mead, G. H. (2011). *G. H. Mead: A Reader.* Ed. Filipe Carreira da Silva. London: Routledge.

Meadwell, Hudson. (2016). "The Rationalist Puzzle of War." *Quality & Quantity* 50, no. 4: 1415–27.

"A Measure of Trust." (2019, September 5). *Nature* 573: 5.

Melander, Erik, Therése Pettersson, and Lotta Themnér. (2016). "Organized Violence, 1989–2015." *Journal of Peace Research* 53, no. 5: 727–42.

Memmi, Albert. (2006). *Decolonization and the Decolonized.* Trans. Robert Bononno. Minneapolis: University of Minnesota Press.

Meneses, Guillermo Alonso and Juan Manuel Avalos González. (2013). "La investigación del fútbol y sus nexus con los estudios de comunicación: Aproximaciones y ejemplos." *Comunicación y Sociedad nueva época* 20: 33–64.

Merritt, Russell. (1983). "Melodrama: Postmortem for a Phantom Genre." *Wide Angle* 5, no. 3: 24–31.

Messner, Michael A. (1990). "When Bodies Are Weapons: Masculinity and Violence in Sport." *International Review for the Sociology of Sport* 25, no. 3: 203–19.

Messner, Michael A. (1997). *Politics of Masculinities: Men in Movements.* Thousand Oaks: Sage.

Meyers, Lawrence. (2014, July 2). "James Bond: Super Spy. Franchise Anchor. Icon of Masculinity." *Breitbart*, www.breitbart.com/big-hollywood/2014/07/02/james-bond-masculine-icon/.

Michels, Robert. (1915). *Political Parties: A Sociological Study of the Oligarchical Tendencies of Modern Democracy.* Trans. Eden and Cedar Paul. London: Jarrold & Sons.

Miguel, Edward, Sebastian M. Saiegh, and Shanker Satyanath. (2011). "Civil War Exposure and Violence." *Economics & Politics* 23, no. 1: 59–73.

Miliband, Ralph. (1969). *The State in Capitalist Society.* New York: Basic Books.

Mill, John Stuart. (1859). *On Liberty*, www.econlib.org/library/Mill/mlLbty3.html.

Mill, John Stuart. (1861). *Considerations on Representative Government*, www.constitution.org/jsm/rep_gov.htm.

Miller, J. D. B. (1981). *The World of States: Connected Essays.* New York: St. Martin's Press.

Miller, J. D. B. (1986). *Norman Angell and the Futility of War: Peace and the Public Mind.* Basingstoke: Macmillan.

Miller, Toby. (1998). *Technologies of Truth: Cultural Citizenship and the Popular Media.* Minneapolis: University of Minnesota Press.

Miller, Toby. (2007). *Cultural Citizenship: Cosmopolitanism, Consumerism, and Television in a Neoliberal Age.* Philadelphia: Temple University Press.

Miller, Toby. (2008). *Makeover Nation: The United States of Reinvention.* Columbus: Ohio State University Press.

Miller, Toby. (2009). *Television Studies: The Basics.* London: Routledge.

Miller, Toby. (2013). "US Imperialism, Sport, and 'The Most Famous Soldier in the War'." *A Companion to Sport.* Ed. David L. Andrews and Ben Carrington. Malden: Blackwell. 229–45.

Miller, Toby. (2020). The Persistence of Violence: Colombian Popular Culture. New Brunswick: Rutgers University Press.

Mills, C. Wright. (1963). *Power, Politics and People: The Collected Essays of C. Wright Mills.* Ed. Irving Louis Horowitz. New York: Oxford University Press.

Milton, John. (1869). *Areopagitica: A Speech of Mr. John Milton for the Liberty of Unlicenc'd Printing, to the Parliament of England.* Ed. Edward Arber. London: Bloomsbury.

Milton, John. (2005). *Paradise Lost.* Oxford: Oxford University Press.

Ministry of Justice. (2019). *Attrition and Progression: Reported Sexual Violence Victimisations in the Criminal Justice System,* www.justice.govt.nz/assets/Documents/Publications/sf79dq-Sexual-violence-victimisations-attrition-and-progression-report-v1.0.pdf?fbclid=IwAR2VYNMPni6mC6-HVJe5KcnRqFqdTzGevrci9jP4eqrXIcPfKq5-FW5abPE.

Mitchell, Alice Miller. (1929). *Children and the Movies.* Chicago: University of Chicago Press.

Moeller, Susan D. (2004). *Media Coverage of Weapons of Mass Destruction.* Center for International and Security Studies at Maryland, https://drum.lib.umd.edu/bitstream/handle/1903/7884/wmdstudy_full.pdf?sequence=1&isAllowed=y.

Moloney, Anastasia. (2015, June 4). "Colombia Approves Femicide Law to Tackle Violence Against Women." *Reuters,* www.reuters.com/article/us-colombia-femicide-idUSKBN0OK22C20150604.

Moloney, Anastasia. (2018, September 12). "Colombia Failing to Fight Child Sexual Exploitation, Officials Admit." *Reuters,* www.reuters.com/article/us-colombia-humantrafficking-youth/colombia-failing-to-fight-child-sexual-exploitation-officials-admit-idUSKCN1LS0I6.

Monkonnen, Eric H. (2001). *Murder in New York City.* Berkeley: University of California Press.

Montaño, John. (2018, August 1). "Las relaciones de 'Madame' con proxenetas israelíes." *El Tiempo,* www.eltiempo.com/colombia/otras-ciudades/quien-es-liliana-del-carmen-campos-puello-alias-madame-249974.

Moore, Lorrie. (2019). "Hard Feelings: A Review of *Lorena.*" *Sewanee Review* 127, no. 3: 600–06.

Morgan, Rachel E. and Jennifer L. Truman. (2018). *Criminal Victimization, 2017.* U.S. Department of Justice, Office of Justice Programs, Bureau of Justice Statistics, www.bjs.gov/content/pub/pdf/cv17.pdf.

Morgenthau, Hans J. (1948). *Politics among Nations: The Struggle for Power and Peace.* New York: Alfred A. Knopf.

Morris, William. (1978). *Stories in Prose, Stories in Verse, Shorter Poems, Lectures and Essays.* Ed. G. D. H. Cole. New York: AMS Press.

Mosca, Gaetano. (1939). *The Ruling Class.* Trans. Hannah D. Kahn. Ed. Arthur Livingston. New York: McGraw-Hill.

Mosco, Vincent. (2004). *The Digital Sublime: Myth, Power, and Cyberspace.* Cambridge, MA: MIT Press.

Moser, Caroline and Cathy McIlwaine. (2000). *Urban Poor Perceptions of Violence and Exclusion in Colombia: Conflict Prevention and Post-Conflict Reconstruction.* Washington: World Bank.

Mosquera, Mabel Valencia and Carlos Ospina Bozzi. (2005). "El abordaje de la problemática de explotación sexual infantil en Cartagena." *Palabra* 6: 137–53.

Nájar, Alberto. (2019, November 19). "Emma Coronel: La controversia en México por la aparición de esposa de 'El Chapo' Guzmán en la serie 'Cartel Crew'." *BBC Mundo*, www.bbc.com/mundo/noticias-america-latina-50468850.

National Coalition Against Domestic Violence. (2019). *Domestic Violence*, www.speakcdn.com/assets/2497/domestic_violence2.pdf.

National Sexual Violence Resource Center. (2019). *Get Statistics: Sexual Assault in the United States*, www.nsvrc.org/statistics.

Newman, Kim. (2000, January 1). "Goldeneye." *Empire*, www.empireonline.com/movies/reviews/goldeneye-review/.

Nietzsche, Friedrich. (2002). *Beyond Good and Evil: Prelude to a Philosophy of the Future*. Trans. Judith Norman. Ed. Rolf-Peter Horstmann and Judith Norman. Cambridge: Cambridge University Press.

Nixon, Robert. (2011). *Slow Violence and the Environmentalism of the Poor*. Cambridge, MA: Harvard University Press.

Nkrumah, Kwame. (1969). *Axioms of KWAME NKRUMAH: Freedom Fighters' Edition*. London: Panaf Books.

Nolasco, Stephanie. (2019, January 5). "Cocaine Godmother's Son Claims 'Cartel Crew' Doesn't Glorify Criminal Lifestyle." *Fox News*, www.foxnews.com/entertainment/cocaine-godmother-griselda-blancos-son-claims-cartel-crew-doesnt-glorify-criminal-lifestyle-were-trying-to-move-on-with-our-lives.

Nolte, John. (2019a, April 29). "Daniel Craig Endorses Terrible Idea of Female James Bond." *Breitbart*, www.breitbart.com/entertainment/2019/04/29/daniel-craig-endorses-terrible-idea-of-female-james-bond/.

Nolte, John. (2019b, November 11). "Woke James Bond Marries Bossy Feminist, Drives Electric Car." *Breitbart*, www.breitbart.com/entertainment/2019/11/11/nolte-woke-james-bond-marries-bossy-feminist-drives-electric-car/.

Norris, Pippa and Ronald Inglehart. (2003). "Public Opinion Among Muslims and the West." *Framing Terrorism: The News Media, the Government, and the Public*. Ed. Pippa Norris, Montague Kern, and Marion Just. New York: Routledge. 203–28.

"Not the Kind of Press They Were After." (2012, April 21). *Economist*, www.economist.com/americas-view/2012/04/21/not-the-kind-of-press-they-were-after.

Nussbaum, Martha C. (1999). *Sex & Social Justice*. New York: Oxford University Press.

O'Brien, Erin, Sharon Hayes, and Belinda Carpenter. (2013). *The Politics of Sex Trafficking: A Moral Geography*. New York: Palgrave Macmillan.

Observatorio Nacional Ciudadano Seguridad, Justicia y Legalidad. (2019). *Reporte sobre delitos de alto impacto*, http://onc.org.mx/wp-content/uploads/2019/10/Reporte-jul19.pdf.

Ojeda, Diana. (2013). "War and Tourism: The Banal Geographies of Security in Colombia's 'Retaking'." *Geopolitics* 18, no. 4: 759–78.

Onwumechili, Chuka. (2007). "Nigeria: Equivocating While Opening the Broadcast Liberalization Gates." *Negotiating Democracy: Media Transformations in*

Emerging Democracies. Ed. Isaac A. Blankson and Patrick D. Murphy. Albany: State University of New York Press. 123–42.

Oquendo, Catalina. (2020, March 26). "El coronavirus no detiene la violencia en Colombia." *El País*, https://elpais.com/internacional/2020-03-26/el-coronavirus-no-detiene-la-violencia-en-colombia.html.

Organización Internacional para las Migraciones. (2015). *Justicia y violencia sexual: Cartilla explicativa de los contenidos de la Ley 1719 de 2014*, https://reposi tory.oim.org.co/bitstream/handle/20.500.11788/1292/COL-OIM0508.pdf;jsessio nid=B33BB9D1498A9D4123917CAD6786B71C?sequence=1.

Organization for Economic Cooperation and Development. (2016). *States of Fragility 2016: Understanding Violence*, http://dx.doi.org/10.1787/9789264267213-en.

Orrego Ramírez, Lina Maria, Jorge Iván Velásquez Restrepo, and Lucas Uribe Lopera. (2010). "Caracterización psicosocial del futbolista perteneciente a la categoría primera 'A' del Fútbol Professional Colombiano." *Pensando Psicología* 6, no. 10: 11–21.

Ortega y Gasset, José. (1930). *The Revolt of the Masses*, http://pinkmonkey.com/dl/library1/revolt.pdf.

Orwell, George. (1944, May 12). "As I Please." *Tribune*, www.orwell.ru/library/articles/As_I_Please/english/eaip_01.

Orwell, George. (1945, December). "The Sporting Spirit." *Tribune*, www.orwell.ru/library/articles/spirit/english/e_spirit.

Orwell, George. (1958). *The Road to Wigan Pier*. Orlando: Harvest.

Overy, Richard. (2020, March 19). "Why the Cruel Myth of the 'Blitz Spirit' is No Model for How to Fight Coronavirus." *Guardian*, www.theguardian.com/commentisfree/2020/mar/19/myth-blitz-spirit-model-coronavirus.

Oxfam. (2009). *La violencia sexual en Colombia: Una arma de guerra*, www.oxfam.org/sites/www.oxfam.org/files/file_attachments/bp-sexual-violence-colombia-sp 3.pdf.

Parekh, Bhikhu. (2008). *A New Politics of Identity: Political Principles for an Interdependent World*. Houndmills: Palgrave Macmillan.

PA Media. (2019, September 23). "Reports of Sexual Assaults on London Underground Soar." *Guardian*, www.theguardian.com/uk-news/2019/sep/23/reports-sexual-assaults-london-underground-soar.

Pareto, Vilfredo. (1976). *Sociological Writings*. Trans. Derick Mirfin. Ed. S. E. Finer. Oxford: Basil Blackwell.

Parkinson, Charles. (2020, March 26). "Three Women Murdered on First Day of Colombia's Coronavirus Lockdown." *Colombia Reports*, https://colombiareports.com/three-women-murdered-on-first-day-of-colombias-coronavirus-lockdown/.

Parsons, Talcott, Robert F. Bales, James Olds, Morris Zelditch, Jr., and Philip E. Slater. (1955). *Family, Socialization and Interaction Process*. Glencoe: Free Press.

"Parents of Slain Army Ranger Tillman: McChrystal Shouldn't Get Top Afghanistan Post." (2009, May 13). *FoxNews*, www.foxnews.com/story/parents-of-slain-army-ranger-tillman-mcchrystal-shouldnt-get-top-afghanistan-post.

Paz, Octavio. (1961). *The Labyrinth of Solitude: Life and Thought in Mexico*. Trans. Lysander Kemp. New York: Grove Press; London: Evergreen Books.

The Peace Alliance. (2015). *Key Statistics on the Challenges of Violence & Crime*, https://peacealliance.org/wp-content/uploads/2013/05/statistics-on-violence-2015.pdf.

Peterson, Jillian and James Densley. (2019, August 4). "Op-Ed: We Have Studied Every Mass Shooting Since 1966. Here's What We've Learned About the Shooters." *Los Angeles Times*, www.latimes.com/opinion/story/2019-08-04/el-paso-dayton-gilroy-mass-shooters-data.

Peterson, V. Spike, ed. (1992). *Gendered States: Feminist (Re)Visions of International Relations Theory.* Boulder: Lynne Rienner.

Pineda Duque, Javier Armando. (2003). *Masculinidades, género y desarrollo: Sociedad civil, machismo y microempresa en Colombia.* Bogotá: Universidad de Los Andes.

Pinker, Steven. (2011). *The Better Angels of Our Nature: Why Violence Has Declined.* New York: Viking.

Piñon, Juan. (2019). "Disruption and Continuity on [sic.] *Telenovela* with the Surge of a New Hybrid Prime-Time Fictional Serial: The Super Series." *Critical Studies in Television: The International Journal of Television Studies* 14, no. 2: 204–21.

Pinter, Harold. (2009). *Various Voices: Sixty Years of Prose, Poetry, Politics 1948–2008.* London: Faber and Faber.

Plato. (1997). *Complete Works.* Ed. John M. Cooper. Assoc. Ed. D. S. Hutchinson. Indianapolis: Hackett Publishing Company.

Polanyi, Karl. (2001). *The Great Transformation: The Political and Economic Origins of Our Time.* Boston: Beacon Press.

Polmar, Norman and Thomas B. Allen. (1997). *The Encyclopedia of Espionage.* New York: Gramercy.

Popovski, Vesselin, Gregory M. Reichberg, and Nicholas Turner, eds. (2009). *World Religions and Norms of War.* Tokyo: United Nations University Press.

Poulantzas, Nicos. (2008). *The Poulantzas Reader: Marxism, Law and the State.* Ed. James Martin. London: Verso.

"Progress and Challenges of Conflict Minerals." (2018). *The Enough Project*, https://enoughproject.org/wp-content/uploads/Progress-and-challenges-June-2018.pdf.

Puello Sarabia, Cielo Patricia and Erika Paola Ardila Palacio. (2019). "La ciudad erotizada: Análisis discursivo de un blog turístico sobre Cartagena de Indias." *ACTAS ICONO* 14: 166–81.

Pufendorf, Samuel. (1994). *The Political Writings of Samuel Pufendorf.* Trans. Michael J. Seidler. Ed. Craig L. Carr. New York: Oxford University Press.

Pufendorf, Samuel. (2000). *On the Duty of Man and Citizen According to Natural Law.* Trans. Michael Silverthorne. Ed. James Tully. Cambridge: Cambridge University Press.

Puig-i-Abril, Eulàlia and Hernando Rojas. (2018). "Silencing Political Opinions: An Assessment of the Influence of Geopolitical Contexts in Colombia." *Communication Research* 45, no. 1: 55–82.

Pye, Lucien W. (1965). "Introduction: Political Culture and Political Development." *Political Culture and Political Development.* Ed. Lucien W. Pye and Sidney Verba. Princeton: Princeton University Press. 3–26.

Raine, Adrian. (2013). *The Anatomy of Violence: The Biological Roots of Crime.* New York: Pantheon.

Ramírez Murcia, Armando. (2016). "Telenovela y género en Colombia." *Nóesis*: 46–64.

Ramsaye, Terry. (1947). "The Rise and Place of the Motion Picture." *Annals of the American Academy of Political and Social Science* 254: 1–11.

Rand, Ayn. (1975). *The Romantic Manifesto: A Philosophy of Literature*, rev. ed. New York: Signet.

Rawls, John. (1999). *The Law of Peoples with "The Idea of Public Reason Revisited."* Cambridge, MA: Harvard University Press.

Rayas Velasco, Lucía. (2009). *Armadas: Un análisis de género desde el cuerpo de las mujeres combatientes.* Mexico City: Colegio de México.

Red Chilena Contra La Violencia Hacia Las Mujeres. (2018–19). *Dossier informativo: Violencia contra las mujeres en Chile*, www.nomasviolenciacontramujeres. cl/wp-content/uploads/2019/09/DOSSIER-2019-1.pdf.

Reeves, Geoffrey. (1993). *Communications and the "Third World."* London: Routledge.

Reich, Robert. (1999, December 19). "Brain Trusts." *New York Times Book Review*: 10.

Reilly, Tom. (2009, August 30). "Seven 'Sorry' for Bulger Ad." *The Age*, www. theage.com.au/entertainment/seven-sorry-for-bulger-ad-20090830-ge82hi.html.

Richardson, James D., comp. (2004). *A Compilation of the Messages and Papers of the Presidents, Volume 2: James Monroe.* Project Gutenberg, www.gutenberg. org/files/11021/11021-h/11021-h.htm.

Richardson, Reed. (2017, July 27). "Body Count Comeback: Corporate Media Routinely Repeat Pentagon Kill Estimates That Defy Reality." *FAIR*, https://fair.org/home/body-count-comeback/.

Riley, Robin L., Chandra Talpade Mohanty, and Minnie Bruce Pratt, eds. (2008). *Feminism and War: Confronting U.S. Imperialism.* London: Zed Books.

Rincón, Ómar. (2015). "Amamos a Pablo, odiamos a los políticos: Las repercusiones de *Escobar, el patrón del mal.*" *Nueva Sociedad* 255: 94–105.

Rincón, Omar. (2018, July 22). "La narcoficción/El otro lado." *El Tiempo*, www.eltiempo.com/cultura/cine-y-tv/la-narcoficcion-en-mexico-y-colombia-el-otro-lado-de-omar-rincon-246578.

Rincón, Omar. (2019). "TV-violencias: Mejor contados en la ficción que en la información." *Revista de Estudios Hispánicos* 53, no. 1: 187–209.

Roberts, Les, Riyadh Lafta, Richard Garfield, Jamal Khuhairi, and Gilbert Burnham. (2004). "Mortality Before and After the 2003 Invasion of Iraq: Cluster Sample Survey." *The Lancet* 364: 1857–64.

Rogers, Carl R. (1995). *On Becoming a Person: A Therapist's View of Psychotherapy.* Boston: Houghton Mifflin.

Rojas, Cristina. (2002). *Civilization and Violence: Regimes of Representation in Nineteenth-Century Colombia.* Minneapolis: University of Minnesota Press.

Rose, Jacqueline. (2014). *Women in Dark Times.* London: Bloomsbury.

Roszak, Theodore. (1969). *The Making of a Counterculture: Reflections on Technocratic Society and Its Youthful Opposition.* New York: Anchor Books.

Roth, Randolph. (2009). *American Homicide*. Cambridge, MA: The Belknap Press of Harvard University Press.

Rouch, Jean. (2003). *Ciné-Ethnography*. Ed. and Trans. Steve Feld. Minneapolis: University of Minnesota Press.

Rousseau, Jean-Jacques. (1975). *The Social Contract and Discourses*. Trans. G. D. H. Cole. London: JM Dent.

Rowe, David. (1997). "Big Defence: Sport and Hegemonic Masculinity." *Gender, Sport and Leisure: Continuities and Challenges*. Ed. Alan Tomlinson. Aachen: Meyer and Meyer Verlag. 123–33.

Roxborough, Ian. (2015). "The Future of War." *Sociological Forum* 30, no. 2: 459–74.

Roy, Arundhati. (2002). *The Algebra of Infinite Justice*, rev. ed. New Delhi: Penguin Books India.

Rudolfsen, Ida. (2019). "Non-State Conflicts: Trends from 1989 to 2018." *Conflict Trends* 2, www.prio.org/utility/DownloadFile.ashx?id=1859&type=publicationfile.

Rupar, Aaron. (2020, April 3). "Jared Kushner's Ventilator Remarks Contradicted a Government Website. Hours Later, the Site was Changed." *Vox*, www.vox.com/2020/4/3/21207140/jared-kushner-strategic-national-stockpile-ventilators.

Rusbridger, Alan. (2020, March 29). "Amid Our Fear, We're Rediscovering Utopian Hopes of a Connected World." *Guardian*, www.theguardian.com/commentisfree/2020/mar/29/coronavirus-fears-rediscover-utopian-hopes-connected-world.

Rusciano, Frank. (2003). "Framing World Opinion in the Elite Press." *Framing Terrorism: The News Media, the Government, and the Public*. Ed. Pippa Norris, Montague Kern, and Marion Just. New York: Routledge. 159–79.

Russell, Bertrand. (2009). *Political Ideals*. N. p.: Project Gutenberg.

Safire, William. (1994, February 6). "On Language: The Horny Dilemma." *New York Times*: Magazine 10.

Said, Edward W. (1994). *Culture and Imperialism*. New York: Vintage.

Said, Edward W. (2001, October 15). "We All Swim Together." *New Statesman*: 20.

Saiya, Nilay. (2017). "Blasphemy and Terrorism in the Muslim World." *Terrorism and Political Violence* 29, no. 6: 1087–105.

Salazar, Miguel. (2018, September 26). "Soccer and Domestic Violence: When the Beautiful Game Turns Ugly." *The Nation*, www.thenation.com/article/soccer-and-domestic-violence-when-the-beautiful-game-turns-ugly/.

Saldaña, Magdalena and Rachel R. Mourão. (2018). "Reporting in Latin America: Issues and Perspectives on Investigative Journalism in the Region." *International Journal of Press/Politics* 23, no. 3: 299–323.

Salinas Arango, Natalia Andrea. (2018). "Encrucijada de la violencia asociada al fútbol: Entre el desagrado y la complacencia." *Trabajo Social* 20, no. 1: 49–68.

Sandel, Michael J. (1998). *Liberalism and the Limits of Justice*. Cambridge: Cambridge University Press.

Sandel, Michael J. (2007). *The Case against Perfection: Ethics in the Age of Genetic Engineering*. Cambridge, MA: Harvard University Press.

Sarnoff, David. (2004). "Our Next Frontier . . . Transoceanic TV." *Mass Communication and American Social Thought: Key Texts, 1919–1968*. Ed. John Durham Peters and Peter Simonson. Lanham: Rowman & Littlefield. 309–10.

Sartre, Jean-Paul. (2004). "Preface." *The Wretched of the Earth*. Ed. Frantz Fanon. Trans. Richard Philcox. New York: Grove Press. 99–158.

Saunders, David. (1997). *Anti-Lawyers: Religion and the Critics of Law and State*. London: Routledge.

Savanta ComRes. (2019, November 21). *BBC 5 Live, Women's Poll–21st November 2019*, www.comresglobal.com/wp-content/uploads/2019/11/Final-BBC-5-Live-Tables_211119cdh.pdf.

Schaeffer, R. K. (1997). *Understanding Globalization: The Social Consequences of Political, Economic, and Environmental Change*. Lanham: Rowman & Littlefield.

Scheele, Fleur, Esther de Haan, and Vincent Kiezebrink. (2016). *Cobalt Blues: Environmental Pollution and Human Rights Violations in Katanga's Copper and Cobalt Mines*. Good Electronics, www.somo.nl/cobalt-blues/.

Schickel, Richard. (1995, November 27). "Shaky, not Stirring." *Time*, http://content.time.com/time/magazine/article/0,9171,983763,00.html.

Schimmel, Kimberly S., C. Lee Harrington, and Denise D. Bielby. (2007). "Keep Your Fans to Yourself: The Disjuncture between Sport Studies' and Pop Culture Studies' Perspectives on Fandom." *Sport in Society* 10, no. 4: 580–600.

Schlesinger, Philip, R. Emerson Dobash, Russell P. Dobash, and C. Kay Weaver. (1992). *Women Viewing Violence*. London: British Film Institute.

Schmitt, Eric. (2005, January 16). "New U.S. Commander Sees Shift in Military Role in Iraq." *New York Times*: 10.

Schumpeter, Joseph Alois. (1966). *Imperialism & Social Classes: Two Essays*. Trans. Heinz Norden. Cleveland: Meridian Books.

Schutz, Alfred. (1972). *The Phenomenology of the Social World*. Trans. George Walsh and Frederick Lehnert. Evanston: Northwestern University Press.

Scott, Walter. (1805). *The Lay of the Last Minstrel*, http://theotherpages.org/poems/minstrel.

Scurich, Nicholas. (2016). "An Introduction to the Assessment of Violence Risk." *International Perspectives on Violence Risk Assessment*. Ed. Jay P. Singh, Stål Bjørkly, and Seena Fazel. New York: Oxford University Press. 3–15.

Sen, Amartya. (2006). *Identity and Violence: The Illusion of Destiny*. New York: W. W. Norton.

Serrano-Amaya, José Fernando. (2018). *Homophobic Violence in Armed Conflict and Political Transition*. Cham: Palgrave Macmillan.

Shapiro, Michael J. (2001). *For Moral Ambiguity: National Culture and the Politics of the Family*. Minneapolis: University of Minnesota Press.

Shapiro, Michael J. (2015). *War Crimes, Atrocity, and Justice*. Cambridge: Polity Press.

Sharma, Vivek Swaroop. (2015). "A Social Theory of War: Clausewitz and War Reconsidered." *Cambridge Review of International Affairs* 28, no. 3: 327–47.

Sibilia, Paola. (2009). *El hombre postorgánico: Cuerpo, subjetividad y tecnologías digitales*, 2nd ed. Buenos Aires: Fondo de Cultura Económica.

Simmel, Georg. (1949). "The Sociology of Sociability." Trans. Everett C. Hughes. *American Journal of Sociology* 55, no. 3: 254–61.

Simon, Scott and Emma Bowman. (2018, June 16). "Domestic Violence Expert Resigns from NFL Players Association Commission." *NPR*, www.npr.org/2018/

06/16/620314505/domestic-violence-expert-resigns-from-nfl-players-association-commission.

Singer, Dorothy G. and Jerome L. Singer. (2001). "Introduction: Why a Handbook on Children and the Media?" *Handbook of Children and the Media*. Ed. Dorothy G. Singer and Jerome L. Singer. Thousand Oaks: Sage Publications. xi–xvii.

Sjoberg, Laura. (2013). *Gendering Global Conflict: Toward a Feminist Theory of War*. New York: Columbia University Press.

Sklar, Robert. (1992). *City Boys: Cagney, Bogart, Garfield*. Princeton: Princeton University Press.

Small Arms Survey. (2016, November). "A Gendered Analysis of Violent Deaths." *Research Notes* 63, www.smallarmssurvey.org/fileadmin/docs/H-Research_Notes/SAS-Research-Note-63.pdf.

Smith, Anthony D. (2000). *The Nation in History: Historiographical Debates about Ethnicity and Nationalism*. Oxford: Polity Press.

Soderlund, Gretchen. (2011). "The Rhetoric of Revelation: Sex Trafficking and the Journalistic Exposé." *Humanity: An International Journal of Human Rights, Humanitarianism, and Development* 2, no. 2: 193–211.

Solanas, Valerie. (1983). *The Scum Manifesto*, www.markfoster.net/struc/the_scum_manifesto.pdf.

Solomon, Norman. (2001, December). "Media War without End." *Z Magazine.*

Sorel, George. (2004). *Reflections on Violence*. Ed. Jeremy Jennings. Trans. Thomas Ernest Hulme, rev. Jeremy Jennings. Cambridge: Cambridge University Press.

Stack, Peter. (1995, November 17). "Goldeneye." *San Francisco Chronicle*, www.sfgate.com/movies/article/FILM-REVIEW-New-Bond-More-Action-Than-Style-3019862.php.

Stack, Steven. (2003). "Media Coverage as a Risk Factor in Suicide." *Journal of Epidemiology and Community Health* 57, no. 4: 238–40.

Staiger, Janet. (2005). *Media Reception Studies*. New York: New York University Press.

Иосиф Сталин. [Stalin, Joseph]. (1946). "Stalin on Art and Culture." *Revolutionary Democracy*, www.northstarcompass.org/nsc0306/stalin.htm.

Steiker, Carol S. and Jordan M. Steiker, eds. (2019). *Comparative Capital Punishment*. Cheltenham: Edward Elgar.

Stevens, Evelyn P. (1973). "Marianismo: The Other Face of *Machismo* in Latin America." *Female and Male in Latin America: Essays*. Ed. Ann Pescatello. Pittsburgh: University of Pittsburgh Press. 89–101.

Stevis-Grindneff, Matina. (2020, April 5). "The Rising Heroes of the Coronavirus Era? Nations' Top Scientists." *New York Times*, www.nytimes.com/2020/04/05/world/europe/scientists-coronavirus-heroes.html.

Stewart, Frances. (2002). "Root Causes of Violent Conflict in Developing Countries." *British Medical Journal* 324, no. 7333: 342–45.

Still, George Frederic. (1902, April 12). "Some Abnormal Psychical Conditions in Children: The Goulstonian Lectures." *Lancet* 1: 1008–12, 1077–82, 1163–68.

Strange, Susan. (1979). "The Management of Surplus Capacity: Or How Does Theory Stand Up to Protectionism 1970s Style?" *International Organization* 33, no. 3: 303–34.

Strange, Susan. (1998). *The Retreat of the State: The Diffusion of Power in the World Economy*. Cambridge: Cambridge University Press.

Strasser, Ulrike and Heidi Tinsman. (2010). "It's a Man's World? World History Meets the History of Masculinity, Latin American Studies, for Instance." *Journal of World History* 21, no. 1: 75–96.

Suárez Pinzón, Ivonne. (2015). "Violencia de género y violencia sexual del conflicto armado colombiano." *Cambios y Permanencias* 6: 173–203.

Suárez Serrano, Chema. (2016). "El periodismo en los conflictos armados del siglo XXI: Entre las nuevas tecnologías y las amenazas de siempre." *Revista del Instituto Español de Estudios Estratégicos* 8, http://revista.ieee.es/index.php/ieee/article/view/307.

Sundberg, Ralph, Kristine Eck, and Joakim Kreutz. (2012). "Introducing the UCDP Non-State Conflict Dataset." *Journal of Peace Research* 49, no. 2: 351–62.

Surgeon General's Scientific Advisory Committee on Television and Social Behavior. (1971). *Television and Growing Up: The Impact of Televised Violence*. Report to the Surgeon General, U.S. Public Health Service. Washington: U.S. Government Printing Service.

Swanson, Jeffrey W., Richard J. Bonnie, and Paul S. Appelbaum. (2015). "Getting Serious About Reducing Suicide: More 'How' and Less 'Why'." *Journal of the American Medical Association* 314, no. 21: 2229–30.

Thompson, E. P. (1971). "The Moral Economy of the English Crowd in the Eighteenth Century." *Past & Present* 50: 76–136.

Tillman, Kevin. (2006, October 19). "After Pat's Birthday." *Truthdig*, www.truthdig.com/articles/after-pats-birthday-2/.

"Tillman Killed in Afghanistan." (2004, April 23). *Sports Illustrated*, http://sportsillustrated.cnn.com/2004/football/nfl/04/23/tillman.killed/.

Tillman, Mary. (2017, December 6). "President and Congress Ignored My Family's Warnings About McChrystal." *HuffPost*, www.huffpost.com/entry/president-and-congress-sw_b_681919.

Tillman, Mary and Narda Zacchino. (2008). *Boots on the Ground at Dusk: My Tribute to Pat Tillman*. New York: Modern Times.

Tilly, Charles. (2008). *The Politics of Collective Violence*. Cambridge: Cambridge University Press.

Tippins, Stephen B., Jr. (2012, October 17). "007's Masculine Mystique." *American Conservative*, www.theamericanconservative.com/articles/007s-masculine-mystique/.

Tolstoy, Leo. (1990). *Government is Violence: Essays on Anarchism and Pacifism*. Ed. David Stephens. London: Phoenix Press.

Tracinski, Robert. (2015, November 6). "Why We Need James Bond." *The Federalist*, https://thefederalist.com/2015/11/06/why-we-need-james-bond/.

Tulloch, John. (1990). *Television Drama: Agency, Audience and Myth*. London: Routledge.

Tulloch, John and Marian Tulloch. (1993). "Understanding TV Violence: A Multifaceted Cultural Analysis." *Nation, Culture, Text: Australian Cultural and Media Studies*. Ed. Graeme Turner. London: Routledge. 211–45.

Uber. (2019). *US Safety Report 2017–2018*, www.uber-assets.com/image/upload/v1575580686/Documents/Safety/UberUSSafetyReport_201718_FullReport.pdf?mod=article_inline.

Ueda, Michiko, Kota Mori, and Tetsuya Matsubayashi. (2014). "The Effects of Media Reports of Suicides by Well-Known Figures Between 1989 and 2010 in Japan." *International Journal of Epidemiology* 43, no. 2: 623–29.

Unger, Roberto Mangabeira. (1987). *Plasticity into Power: Comparative Historical Studies on the Institutional Conditions of Economic and Military Success: Variations on Themes of Politics, a Work in Constructive Social Theory.* Cambridge: Cambridge University Press.

United Nations. (1993). *Declaration on the Elimination of Violence against Women,* www.un.org/documents/ga/res/48/a48r104.htm.

United Nations Development Program. (2004). *Human Development Report 2004: Cultural Liberty in Today's Diverse World,* http://hdr.undp.org/en/content/human-development-report-2004.

United Nations Office on Drugs and Crime. (2014). *Global Study on Homicide 2013,* www.unodc.org/documents/data-and-analysis/statistics/GSH2013/2014_GLOBAL_HOMICIDE_BOOK_web.pdf.

United Nations Office on Drugs and Crime. (2017). *Better Data to Monitor Violence, Trafficking, Corruption and Access to Justice,* www.unodc.org/documents/data-and-analysis/Crime-statistics/Brochure_goal16_2017_web.pdf.

United Nations Population Fund. (2013). *The Role of Data in Addressing Violence against Women,* https://unfpa.org/sites/default/files/resource-pdf/finalUNFPA_CSW_Book_20130221_Data.pdf.

United States Government Accountability Office. (2018). *Conflict Minerals.* GAO-18–457, www.gao.gov/assets/700/692851.pdf.

U.S. Atomic Energy Commission. (1954). *United States Atomic Energy Commission in the Matter of J. Robert Oppenheimer,* https://archive.org/stream/unitedstatesatom007206mbp/unitedstatesatom007206mbp_djvu.txt.

U.S. Department of Justice–Federal Bureau of Investigation. (2018). *Hate Crime Statistics, 2017,* https://ucr.fbi.gov/hate-crime/2017.

Vásquez, Juan Gabriel. (2013). *The Sound of Things Falling.* New York: Riverhead.

Vázquez Montalbán, Manuel. (1987). "Barça, el ejército de un país desarmado." *Catalonia* 1: 45.

Villota Galeano, Fabián Felipe. (2017). "Identidad nacional colombiana: Discursos, recurrencias y desafíos en contextos de globalización." *Textos y Sentidos* 15: 47–70.

Vincent, Isabel. (2019, November 16). "El Chapo's Wife Emma Coronel Aispuro Makes Classy Debut on on [*sic*] VH1's 'Cartel Crew'." *New York Post,* https://nypost.com/2019/11/16/el-chapos-wife-emma-coronel-aispuro-makes-classy-debut-on-on-vh1s-cartel-crew/.

Violence Policy Center. (2018). *American Roulette: Murder-Suicide in the United States,* 6th ed., http://vpc.org/studies/amroul2018.pdf.

Violence Policy Center. (2019a). *When Men Murder Women: An Analysis of 2017 Homicide Data,* http://vpc.org/studies/wmmw2019.pdf.

Violence Policy Center. (2019b). *Black Homicide Victimization in the United States: An Analysis of 2016 Homicide Data,* http://vpc.org/studies/blackhomicide19.pdf.

Violence Policy Center. (2019c). *Hispanic/Latino Suicide in California,* www.vpc.org/studies/CAlatinosuicide.pdf.

Virilio, Paul. (1989). *War and Cinema: The Logistics of Perception.* Trans. Patrick Camiller. London: Verso.

Viveros, Mara. (2013). "Género, raza y nación: Los réditos políticos de la masculinidad blanca en Colombia." *Maguaré* 27, no. 1: 71–104.

Voltaire. (2000). *Political Writings*. Ed. David Williams. Cambridge: Cambridge University Press.

Von Clausewitz, Carl. (1989). *On War*. Trans. and Ed. Michael Howard and Peter Paret. Princeton: Princeton University Press.

von der Lippe, Berit and Rune Ottosen, eds. (2016). *Gendering War and Peace Reporting: Some Insights–Some Missing Links*. Göteborg: NORDICOM.

von Goethe, Johann Wolfgang. (2013). *The Sorrows of Young Werther and Selected Writings*. Trans. Catherine Hunter. New York: Penguin.

Wahab, Siraj. (2007, May 17). "Islamophobia Worst Form of Terrorism." *Arab News*, www.arabnews.com/node/298472.

Wahl, G. and L. J. Wertheim. (1998). "Paternity Ward." *Sports Illustrated* 88, no. 18: 62–71.

Wallas, Graham. (1967). *The Great Society: A Psychological Analysis*. Lincoln: University of Nebraska Press.

Walzer, Michael. (2006). *Just and Unjust Wars: A Moral Argument with Historical Illustrations*, 4th ed. New York: Basic Books.

Ward, Michael D. and David R. Davis. (1992). "Sizing Up the Peace Dividend: Economic Growth and Military Spending in the United States, 1948–1996." *American Political Science Review* 86, no. 3: 748–55.

Wartella, Ellen. (1996). "The History Reconsidered." *American Communication Research: The Remembered History*. Ed. Everette E. Dennis and Ellen Wartella. Mahwah: Lawrence Erlbaum. 169–80.

Waters, Hannah. (2018, Summer). "How the U.S. Government Is Aggressively Censoring Climate Science." *Audubon*, www.audubon.org/magazine/summer-2018/how-us-government-aggressively-censoring-climate.

Watson, Alison M. (2004). "Seen But Not Heard: The Role of the Child in International Political Economy." *New Political Economy* 9, no. 1: 3–21.

Weber, Max. (1946). *From Max Weber: Essays in Sociology*. Trans. and Ed. H. H. Gerth and C. Wright Mills. New York: Free Press.

Weber, Max. (1981). "Some Categories of Interpretive Sociology." Trans. E. E. Graber. *Sociological Quarterly* 22, no. 2: 151–80.

Weber, Max. (1992). *The Protestant Ethic and the Spirit of Capitalism*. Trans. Talcott Parsons. London: Routledge.

White, Josh. (2005, May 4). "Army Withheld Details About Tillman's Death." *Washington Post*: A3.

Wilkins, Brett. (2020, February 10). "The Beasts and the Bombings: Reflecting on Dresden, February 1945." *Common Dreams*, www.commondreams.org/views/2020/02/10/beasts-and-bombings-reflecting-dresden-february-1945.

Williams, Raymond. (1977). *Marxism and Literature*. Oxford: Oxford University Press.

Wills, Maria E. (2011). *La memoria histórica desde la perspectiva de género: Conceptos y herramientas*. Bogotá: Grupo de Memoria Histórica.

Wittfogel, Karl A. (1967). *Oriental Despotism: A Comparative Study of Total Power*. New Haven: Yale University Press.

Wittgenstein, Ludwig. (1965). "I: A Lecture on Ethics." *The Philosophical Review* 74, no. 1: 3–12.

Wolf, Eric R. (2010). *Europe and the People Without History*. Berkeley: University of California Press.

"Wonder Women and Macho Men." (2015, August 22). *Economist*, www.econo mist.com/news/americas/21661800-latin-american-women-are-making-great-strides-culture-not-keeping-up-wonder-women-and.

Worden, Minky, ed. (2008). *China's Great Leap: The Beijing Games and Olympian Human Rights Challenges*. New York: Seven Stories Press.

World Health Organization. (2002). *World Report on Violence and Health*, www. who.int/.violence_injury_prevention/violence/world_report/en.

World Health Organization. (2013). *Global and Regional Estimates of Violence against Women: Prevalence and Health Effects of Intimate Partner Violence and Non-Partner Sexual Violence*, https://apps.who.int/iris/bitstream/handle/10665/85239/9789241564625_eng.pdf;jsessionid=86111B4E0593CB6A8436BD90752 DB2F4?sequence=1.

World Health Organization. (2017). *Violence against Women*, www.who.int/news-room/fact-sheets/detail/violence-against-women.

World Health Organization. (2018). *Global Status Report on Road Safety 2018*, www.who.int/violence_injury_prevention/road_safety_status/2018/en/.

Yardi, Sarita and Danah Boyd. (2010). "Dynamic Debates: An Analysis of Group Polarization Over Time on Twitter." *Bulletin of Science, Technology and Society* 30, no. 5: 316–27.

Young, Iris Marion. (2000). *Inclusion and Democracy*. New York: Oxford University Press.

Zimbardo, Philip. (2007). *The Lucifer Effect: Understanding How Good People Turn Evil*. New York: Random House.

Zinn, Howard. (2003). "Introduction." *Target Iraq: What the News Media Didn't Tell You*. Norman Solomon and Reese Erlich. New York: Context Books. vii–xiii.

Zirin, Dave. (2005, October 6). "Pat Tillman, Our Hero." *The Nation*, www.thenation.com/article/archive/pat-tillman-our-hero/.

Index